Salute me when you see me!

Salute me when you see me!

An affectionate portrait by his son of the father he never knew

by
Michael Fass

First published in Great Britain in 2016
Second Edition 2017
Third Edition 2019

by Michael Fass c/o The Coach House, Old Gore,
Ross on Wye, Herefordshire, HR9 7QT

Printed by Biddles Books Ltd
www.biddles.co.uk

Cover design by John Fass

ISBN printed book 978-1-9998156-6-0

Dedication

This book is dedicated to my beloved children and grandchildren who, I am confident, will keep the story of my father alive

Acknowledgements

My thanks to all those who have helped me to complete this book including: the Archivists at Rugby School and the Staff College, Camberley - now at Shrivenham - who provided details of school reports and the Army Lists for 1939 and 1944; Hugh Boscowan at RHQ, Coldstream Guards for his help with 32nd Brigade National Archives data; L/Sgts Clowes and Gwillym at RHQ, Welsh Guards for sight of the War Diaries of the First Battalion for May and June 1944; Robby Dundas for reminiscences of her service at Norfolk House; John Fass for the cover design; Serena Fass for photographs; David Logan for his help with Corpus Christi, Oxford data; Jacques Mathenet for information about his father; John Morton and Leonora Nokes for information about the Fass family and Tom Pearson for his advice about the RMC and my father's early military career.

Last, for my loving wife Iola's forbearance not only towards the production of this book but also for a lifetime of listening to the story told here.

Contents

Introduction

The title of this memoir - *Salute me when you see me* - is taken from the text of a telegram that my father sent to his brother in law, Michael Verey, who was serving with the Warwickshire Yeomanry in North Africa at the time. It was on the occasion of my father's promotion to Lieutenant- Colonel on the D-Day invasion planning staff, code-named *Overlord*. Michael had written to congratulate him. The telegram is dated 10th May 1943. Promotion to Colonel meant putting on the red tabs of the General Staff and my mother always maintained that he was one of the youngest to be eligible to do so in London at that time. My father's response represented his ambition to lead his Welsh Guardsmen back up the Mall to Buckingham Palace after the Trooping of the Colour on HM the King's official birthday, a privilege allowed only to officers serving in His Majesty's Household Division of Foot Guards. In November 1940 he had written to Michael:

> 'May the next year see this business settled and you immaculate in a pinstripe and red carnation journeying into the City whilst I go rolling up the Mall all bearskin and gold braid'.

Michael told me of my father driving him in the family car to Reading Station on New Year's Eve 1939 for Michael to re-join his Regiment after they had spent Christmas together at Bridge House, Twyford, the home of my father's parents-in-law. It was the start of Michael's journey to the Middle East and six years of war without home leave - as he would often remind us! The two young men sang the songs of the day out loud as they drove through the darkness and parted from each other in good spirits. They were never to meet again.

My father was not able to fulfil his ambition to march at the head of his troops up the Mall and from this distance in time it is not possible to provide a proper account of - or to give full justice to – his short life. The events that I relate all happened too long ago, either before I was born or very soon afterwards. My father died just eight days after my birth. He had crossed to Normandy with the Guards Armoured Division on or about the 21st June 1944, fifteen days after the first landings in France. I was born at Pound Cottage, Sonning, on the 22nd June and he was killed near to Cheux outside of the city of Caen on the 30th June. There was never going to have been an opportunity for him to meet with me or I with him.

He was well aware of the risks that he was taking when he insisted on re-joining his Regiment after nine months working as a GSO1 (General Staff Officer Grade 1) on the Operations and Intelligence Liaison staff at COSSAC (Chief of Staff Supreme Allied Command) at its headquarters at Norfolk House, St James Square in London. Here he was responsible, amongst other duties, for the enemy's order of battle, their quality and their numbers. He knew precisely what a front-line commander could expect across the English Channel. By the 30th June, the day of his death, eighteen lieutenant-colonels commanding battalions had been killed and senior army officers were becoming increasingly concerned at these losses (Beevor).

By the time of his death aged 33, my father had not been able to realise all of the opportunities that life might have offered to him had he lived, but in his short life he had certainly fulfilled some of them. His time at COSSAC and his part in the planning of *Overlord*, the D-Day invasion of Normandy, was the pinnacle of his career. At the same time, after a somewhat racy lifestyle as a young officer in the pre-war British Army, he had settled down to married life with his wife, Elizabeth, my mother, who clearly adored him, and their two daughters, my elder sisters, Serena (born 1938) and Ginny (born 1941).

The war-time life of my parents was rackety, which was a common experience at that time. My father was continually away on courses, in training posts, with the battalions of his Regiment or in appointments on the Staff. My mother was either stuck with her parents at their home at

Bridge House, Twyford in Berkshire or joining him for short reunions when she could. Their greatest war-time concerns were about being together, their children, food and getting pregnant again, in that order!

The quality and volume of record keeping in the British Army during the war was not of the highest order, which was throughout the time that my father experienced rapid promotion. It was obviously not a priority and there was too much moving about between different units and postings for clerical systems to catch up. In addition, Household Division officer records were destroyed by V-bombing in 1944, so that a formal record of my father's career progress, his annual reports and achievements, for example, on training courses, have almost all disappeared.

It may be of interest for readers to know that whilst I have read any number of books written about the Second World War, I have found that they are written mainly either by writers concerned with grand strategy, for example, Churchill's war leadership, or by young officers or soldiers in junior ranks at Platoon and Company level. There appear to be very few books written by individuals of my father's rank or specific wartime record with the exception of Martin Lindsay's *So few got through;* Joe Vandeleur's *A Soldier's Story* and Denis Forman's *To Reason Why*. Either the men in these ranks were simply too busy commanding their units to write up their diaries or they belonged to a culture that was reluctant to share with others what they had experienced, or both.

What remains however, at least until the start of the war, suggests an ambitious and successful soldier who attended to his regimental and other military duties and who made the most of the many sporting and other recreational opportunities available to a young man before the war without much means.

The memoir that follows makes no pretence of military expertise, except of the arm-chair variety. Although I too served in the military for a brief period, it was as a volunteer in the County Yeomanry, probably the most leisurely of all military arms, except when there is hard fighting to be done. I was fortunate that I was never obliged to fire a shot in anger and, in reflecting on my father's success as a soldier, I am very well aware of my deficiencies in that department.

It has not been easy therefore to find a way into my father's story except for the existence of a few ephemeral clues left behind by him from all those years ago.

I have the extravagant number of no less than eight Godparents, three of whom were female and five male. Some of these were selected jointly by my parents before his death, but others I acquired as a direct result of it. For example, Robby Dundas worked for my father at Norfolk House, Headquarters of COSSAC; Horace Noble, Scots Guards, was the machine gun officer of a Guards Brigade in which my father was Brigade Major; Joe Vandeleur commanded the 3rd Battalion, Irish Guards in Normandy, the neighbouring battalion to my father's Welsh Guards in 32nd Guards Brigade and General Jock Whitefoord was his superior at COSSAC. One way to tell my father's story has been through the lens of their involvement in his life. However, stories relating to events that took place more than 70 years ago and about an individual born in 1911 are inevitably both partial and incomplete.

The story that I tell is mainly second and third hand but I recall a wise pastoral counsellor once telling me that he had never met anyone in his long experience who possessed such an extraordinary sense of the presence of an individual whom they had never met. I never met my father but I have always felt that I have had a close and positive relationship with him and that I have known him well.

The memoir is written as a result of this relationship conducted in my thoughts; before the time comes when I shall lose this faculty and when the memories of those who knew and loved him so much, have gone completely. However, the reader should be aware of the dangers of projection. That is, the risk that I have projected onto my father ideas, feelings and attitudes that are my own and not his. This is *my* memoir of the father I never met and it is therefore *my* interpretation of the events of his life in those far off times and not his own. Any misrepresentations of his character and achievements that appear in it are therefore my responsibility alone. Likewise, any factual inaccuracies in the narrative or errors in family or military history or practice.

One further point. When reading the letters between my father and mother

I have been aware of the danger of intruding into their lives together in which I had only a walk-on part at the very end of my father's life. When they were apart during war time they wrote to each other every day unless it was impossible for my father to do so because of the service. All the evidence from their correspondence points towards the fact of the great love that they had for each other. If problems arose between them these were almost always caused by the war which covered five of the seven years of their short marriage. As many others have remarked upon about those years, it was not at all easy for anyone trying to carry on a loving and supportive relationship, often *in absentia*.

Throughout the first four years of war my father was away from home – wherever that was – most of his time, but not abroad. While my parents often commented on those who had *gone away,* which was a euphemism for his colleagues and their friends being posted to fighting units overseas, my father was not sent to the battlefront until the very end of his life although he was often advised to prepare himself for it. His skills were in demand in other ways as this memoire describes. Occasional weekends and odd moments together were all that my parents knew and inevitably this caused tensions that were played out in their letters to each other. However, throughout these difficult times when all they wanted was to be together, they never failed to communicate their affection for one another and for their two children, my sisters Serena and Ginny. Knowing as I do that their marriage would end with my father's premature death, in retrospect theirs was a most poignant correspondence.

Another way of telling the story of his life, service and death has been its recording on no less than seven memorials to those who lost their lives in World War II. They represent a number of milestones in his life and mark his death. His name is on the memorial statue to the boys of West Downs killed in the two World Wars which once stood in the school's memorial garden at Winchester, now re-located to Slimbridge Wildfowl Sanctuary in Gloucestershire. The names of 82 boys are recorded on the Memorial of whom 59 – or almost a complete school full - were killed in World War Two.

This Memorial is in the form of a bronze statue of a boy sculpted by

Kathleen Scott, the widow of Captain Robert Falcon Scott of the Antarctic whose son Peter was at West Downs with my father and has the words *Here Am I, Send Me* inscribed on its base. These words from the book of the prophet Isaiah have both haunted and inspired me throughout my life.

My father's name appears on the war memorials at Rugby School and at the Royal Military Academy, Sandhurst. There is a window dedicated to his memory in the Parish church at St Michael's, Inkpen in Berkshire, the village in the country where he and his parents lived - and his name is on its Roll of Honour. The window was designed by my mother and her father Lt. Col. Henry Verey, DSO, my maternal grandfather, and is inspired by the Italian Renaissance. It depicts St Michael & All Angels triumphant and has inscribed at its foot the words:

> '*In proud and loving memory of Lt-Col John Ernest Fass, killed in Normandy on the 30th June 1944 when in command of the 1st Battalion Welsh Guards, aged 33.*'

His gravestone stands in the Commonwealth War Graves Cemetery at St Manvieu, close to where he was killed near the village of Cheux, on the outskirts of Caen in Normandy. Here his body lies in peaceful surroundings side by side with the other Welsh guardsmen who were killed at the same time as himself, whose soldierly qualities he admired so much. His name is carved on the War Memorial at Sonning, the Thames-side village where he and my mother had bought a house in 1943 close to his parents in law shortly before he left for France in 1944. Finally, there is a memorial plaque in the Welsh Guards side-chapel on the south side of the Guards Chapel at Wellington Barracks in Birdcage Walk, London bearing the same inscription as that in Inkpen Church. No one has been more memorialised than my father!

My father left behind the merest fragments of his life. A few letters from brother officers who wrote to my mother at the time of his death, both known to her and from strangers who felt moved to communicate with her; the official marks of his studentship at Sandhurst and letters to his mother Winnie during the time of his service in Palestine and Egypt in the 1930s. In the war years, I have relied mainly on his correspondence with his wife Elizabeth, my mother. Photographic materials were severely restricted in wartime so that there is little to show for his rapid promotion on the staff and his undoubted successes in handling troops during the war years. I have used mainly private papers with some materials coming from the National Archives at Kew in London.

As a matter of record, in 1947 my mother re-married and the family moved from Sonning outside Reading to Oakley Green, near Windsor, still in Berkshire. My mother had known Guy Stanton as a young woman when he had lived at Sharrow Bay on Ullswater close to the homes of her Hasell cousins at Dacre and Dalemain in Cumberland where her family spent their holidays each summer.

Uncle Guy, as my much-loved step-father became known, was a very fine scholar and outstanding all-round athlete and sportsman with a Double Blue from Oxford. At the beginning of the war he was working for his family firm of steelmakers in Sheffield managing a night shift that made engine blocks for Spitfires. As this was vital war work he was not allowed to join up at once although he had learned to fly at University. However, as RAF losses mounted, he volunteered as a Pilot Officer and flew Beaufighters from the RAF's Middle East base on the coast outside Cairo.

He was shot down by an Italian warship during a bombing sortie in the Dodecanese and, after a year-long and traumatic journey up the Italian archipelago as a POW, was transferred to Germany and held at Stalag Luft II, the RAF camp at Sagen in Poland. He participated in the terrible *long march* westwards towards the Allied lines in March 1945 and was eventually airlifted back to Britain where he stayed for a year in a convalescence hospital while he recovered his health. He worked in London after the war and was the father of my youngest sister Henrietta. He died in 1958.

Finally, so much has been thought about and written of the circumstances of my father's ill-timed death – with all its consequences for the life of my mother, my sisters, myself, his family and his friends - that I wanted to write something about his well-led and vibrant *life*.

His story is told in chronological order, that is from boy to man to senior staff officer and finally to commanding officer that is also the story's ending. He had a very short life by today's standards of longevity but one that was full of spirit and achievement.

On a final note, and as his story ends, I have reflected on its meaning and have concluded that like most of us my father had to make choices about the way he would live and die. He had to reconcile his professional life in the Army with his personal life with his wife and family; his ambition for success on the Staff with his duty of service to his Regiment and, at the very end, his decision to go to France and fight with the alternative of staying on the staff at SHAEF (Supreme Headquarters Allied Expeditionary Force) where he expected to be welcomed back by the many friends that he had made there from the COSSAC days.

He chose service and sacrifice and I am intensely proud that this is what gives his life its ultimate meaning.

I salute him always.

Chapter One
ANTECEDENTS

My father was born on the 27th April 1911 at Hans Place, London. He was named John Ernest. His mother Winifred, always known as *Winnie*, nee Neame, was the eldest daughter of Harding Neame Esq. of Kent who married a Miss Annie Cotterill. Both the Neame and Cotterill families were well known in that County. One branch of it owned and managed the Shepherd Neame Brewery in Faversham. The other, my grandmother's branch, managed the Scandinavian timber importation trade into Britain over the South Coast ports. This trade collapsed at the start of the First World War when the Allies mined the Skagerrak Canal to prevent the German Fleet using it to provide access from their naval base at Kiel to the North Sea, and the route was blocked for its duration.

Winnie (born 1881) was the eldest of three sisters. Of her sisters, Doris (born 1882) married an officer of the Loyal North Lancashire Regiment, Patrick Magill; Gwen (born 1883) married Sir Thomas Wrightson of Neasham Hall, Eryholme in the County of Durham whose family owned and managed Head Wrightson, engineers in Darlington and Middlesbrough. Their second son, Peter, my father's first cousin, was to become his greatest friend with whom he spent much of every holidays.

Oliver, the youngest of the Wrightson boys, always known as *Nod*, was a junior officer of the 5th Coldstream Guards serving in Normandy. He was on duty at 32nd Guards Brigade Headquarters when the news that my father had been killed was received on the radio on the night on the 30th June 1944 and was the first member of the family to learn of his death..

Monica (born 1888), the youngest of the four sisters and always known as *Bar*, married Sir Charles Mander paint manufacturers and philanthropists of Wolverhampton. There was one brother, Lionel (born 1897), who served in the Coldstream Guards, a family tradition of service in the Household Division that my father was to emulate. The Neame sisters shared a most particular characteristic which was that they believed that life should be *fun* and lived to the full. Joie de vivre was their motto and their houses were always places that were full of laughter, sometimes at the expense of those with less frivolous natures than themselves. They were accomplished mimics and practical jokers and they had the knack of getting along with people, one of my father's most notable qualities.

Winnie was known as *poor* Winnie because, whilst she was the eldest of the Neame sisters, she was the last to be married and her family had despaired that she ever would be. She was twenty six years old on her wedding day in 1907 and her family continued to refer to her as *poor Winnie* even after this event. On the day of her marriage her husband to be, Herbert Ernest Fass, my paternal grandfather, also born in 1881, advised her that she would be marrying *a creaking door!*

My father's father, Herbert Ernest had a very different pedigree. He was the ninth and youngest child of a South African of German origin, Adolphus Fass, who had emigrated to South Africa aged fifteen for health reasons. The wider Fass family has a number of theories about the provenance of Adolphus. These include that he was the son of a professor of mathematics at Leipzig University; that the family originated from Golinow in the province of Pomerania (later Brandenburg), now Goleniow in Poland, or that they came from Brunswick. A great aunt, Aunt Sophie, was always known as *Sophie of Brunswick* to mark her supposed origins in that part of the Holy Roman Empire. This makes some sense as the river Oder (now the Odra) flows into the Baltic at Szczecin (formerly Stettin) on the eastern edge of which is the town of Golinow. Whatever his background, in South Africa Adolphus developed skills in calculating financial odds and in entrepreneurship. He became a successful businessman in the era of Cecil Rhodes and of British imperial expansion in the mid nineteenth century and participated in the development of that country's industry and commerce - in particular the mining industry.

He owned and managed a business in Natal which was similar to the Army & Navy Stores selling household and other goods, including mining equipment, which was delivered to the mines up at Kimberley by wagon from the Port of Durban. These manufactures were first sold to customers on the diamond fields and then on the Rand when gold was found in that region. Natal was a British Colony and at some point in his career it must have been advantageous that he should take up British citizenship. He subsequently moved to Britain, perhaps to represent the South African business interests in London of himself and of his trading partners. Here he set himself up as a *Nabob* and settled with his family at Chalfont St Peter in a large house where he brought up those of his younger children who had not stayed behind in South Africa, including Herbert Ernest who was born in this country.

The source of Ernest's intellect is a matter of conjecture, but sufficient to record that my father's father, my paternal grandfather, was very clever indeed. He was a scholar at Rugby and whilst only a commoner at Corpus Christi College, Oxford, he was awarded a First Class degree in Jurisprudence in 1903, the only one of that year in the Oxford Law Faculty. Afterwards he applied for a life-time fellowship of All Souls, for which he was one of only two candidates, but was beaten to it by Lord Halifax, later known as the *Holy Fox* who was Chamberlain's Foreign Secretary in the 1930s and in Churchill's first war cabinet of May 1940. My father may well have inherited some of his father's intellectual ability.

Ernest was not the businessman that his father had been and initially practised as a lawyer at the London Bar. After losing a particularly irksome civil case which was about a dispute in the London Docks, he opted for a different life and joined the Civil Service. He served first at the Department of Education and at the Board of Trade before settling into the Treasury. He took part in the financial negotiations at the conferences of both Versailles (1919) and Locarno (1924) and can be seen in a photograph standing behind Prime Minister Lloyd George on the steps of the conference. In June 1922 he went with the Prime Minster to France for a meeting in Calais to discuss reparations that was attended by Lord Curzen the Foreign Secretary, Austin Chamberlain, the Colonial Secretary, Field Marshall Henry Wilson, the Chief of the

Imperial General Staff and Hankey, the Cabinet Secretary with field Marshalls Foch and Weygand representing the French. Afterwards he worked his way up inside the organisation. He was what we would call a Treasury *mandarin*.

In 1930 the cotton crop of the Sudan, which was ruled by the British, and on which the country's economy depended, failed, partly through the mismanagement of its British colonial administrators. These administrators were selected from amongst the top entrants to the civil service from Oxford and Cambridge so long as they had also been awarded a Blue for cricket. They were superb athletes but their grasp of economics was faulty. Britain was in the grip of a deep recession and when the governor general telegraphed Whitehall asking for more money to see him and the cricket eleven through the year (or at least to the end of the cricketing season!) the Treasury refused his request. The only offer that the Treasury was prepared to make was the dispatch of one Ernest Fass Esq, OBE, CB who would take the title of Financial Secretary of the Sudan and - between the lines - sort these sportsmen out!

My grandfather arrived in Khartoum in July 1931. His first act was to cut the salaries of the colonial cricketers by 10% per year, thereby earning their lifelong hatred. Next, as a trusted Treasury man, he re-negotiated the sale of the following year's Sudanese cotton crop with the government of Egypt (also run by the British imperial power) and three years later, the finances of the Sudan were returned to health. Ernest travelled back to Britain by ship in July 1934 and in the Birthday Honours of June 1935 he was awarded a knighthood (KCMG) by King George V for his services.

The Governor General telegraphed him on his way home:

'For three years we have ridden out the storm with your hand upon the helm and even though calmer waters may be, and we trust are, in sight our regrets are none the less keen that it is to be removed'.

To which Ernest replied:

'It is by her own courage and hard work that Sudan is winning her way through the difficulties caused by the world's troubles, I shall not lightly forget, nor will my wife, many kindnesses received and many friendships we have been allowed to make'.

He was now Sir Ernest Fass and *poor Winnie* was Lady Fass. Somewhere in my father's character must have been that pinch of ruthlessness which is one of the attributes of a successful civil servant and soldier.

Over 50 years later as I came out of St John's Church, Prince's Street in Edinburgh after Sunday service, an old man who was a member of the congregation, came up to me and said angrily: "Are you any relation of that man Fass?" When I replied that I was his grandson, he told me the story of the cricketers and the cotton crop.

Sir Ernest's career staggered onwards for a few more years. In 1938, after the Munich crisis, plans were reluctantly agreed upon by the British government that included the control of the national Press in the event of the outbreak of war. By this time, Ernest had been appointed the Public Trustee. This was the individual who became responsible for a person's assets in the event that they died intestate – that is without making a Will before their death. In that case the Public Trustee representing the State took control. In those days, this happened more frequently than nowadays.

As one of the Government's most senior officials, what we would call - *a safe pair of hands* - Sir Ernest, who knew his way around Whitehall, was appointed shadow Minister of Information, that is, the individual who would be in charge of the censorship of the Press if and when war broke out. Unfortunately, his appointment was leaked to the very same Press that would be censored by him in the future and its members reacted with fury. Who was *this man Fass* and what did he know about newspapers and journalism? A question was put to the Prime Minister at Question Time in the House of Commons that Chamberlain answered feebly. Immediately afterwards Hankey, the Cabinet Secretary, who had offered Sir Ernest the *shadow* position, was obliged to write to him at once saying that if he had ever been appointed, which he had not, the appointment would be withdrawn, which it had been, and he would hear no more about it. A real *Sir Humphrey* moment!

His second wartime appointment was more appropriate. As Public Trustee, Sir Ernest was used to handling assets of money and property and at the beginning of World War II he was, in addition to his other duties, appointed Custodian of Enemy Property. This job was to take over the assets of the Axis powers so that they could not be used against the Allied war effort. For example, there could be a risk that German funds held by its national banks in London could be used to purchase war materials from, for example, neutral Sweden that could then be imported into Germany. All the assets of enemy nationals, mainly German and Italian, were therefore confiscated and held in trust by the British Government, represented by Sir Ernest.

However, this led to an unforeseen consequence. In addition to having their assets confiscated, many of these foreign nationals were arrested and detained in detention camps of which the main one was on the Isle of Man as spy fever swept Britain. Amongst those who were incarcerated were a number of Italian families some of whose members had for many years managed and served on the staff of London's clubland including Boodles, White's and the Reform. On the next occasion on which Sir Ernest visited his club, the Oxford and Cambridge, his acquaintances fell upon him to complain that there was no one to serve their lunch because he had locked them all up! They were released immediately.

He served as Custodian for three years until 1942 and was only replaced when his responsibilities were taken over by the Treasury. Many years after the war had ended the President of the United States of America and Britain's Prime Minister each set up commissions whose task it was to check that the process by which any assets that had been stolen or confiscated by either Allied or Axis governments or forces from German and Italian Jewish victims of the Holocaust during the war, had been properly dealt with at its end. In their final report the commission wrote that:

'As Sir Ernest Fass, the first Custodian of Enemy Property, wrote to Mr. E.H. Hodgson of the Board of Trade on 19th October 1939:

"After the Great War the British Government were accused of having introduced for the first time into international relations a policy of confiscation of private property of enemy subjects for reasons other than reasons connected with the prosecution of the war....It seems to me that this time it is very important to secure that no handle is given to the German Government for a similar accusation" '.
(FCO Historical Branch, No. 13, 1998)

I am pleased to be able to record that my grandfather had behaved honourably.

My father therefore had a somewhat unconventional pedigree and if it is our genetic inheritance that drives us and our subsequent stories more than any other factor, John Ernest could be expected to become an interesting product of his parents.

Chapter Two
CHILDHOOD, WEST DOWNS & RUGBY

Childhood

My father, John Ernest, always known as *Johnny* or *Johnnie*, was born on the 27th April 1911, four years after the marriage of his parents. By this time they already had two daughters, Margaret (born 1907) known as *Peggy* and Mary (born 1909) known as *Maria*. John's younger sister Susan was born in 1912. The family had two homes, one in London at 33, Hans Place, just behind Harrods and the other at Foxhill, Inkpen, outside Newbury in Berkshire. Foxhill was located at the foot of the Berkshire downs and became the family's home during the holidays. This house was where my father and his sisters enjoyed life in the country and where my father first learned to ride, an activity that would become a lifelong passion.

By all accounts he had a happy early childhood that included a hint of bohemianism. Ernest spent the week in his office at the Board of Education or the Treasury whilst Winnie lived in the country. Winnie was no great disciplinarian and whilst their parents stayed in London or Berkshire for part of the summer, the four children went to stay at a house at Hartland Bay in Devon where they were looked after by a governess-nanny and enjoyed a good deal of freedom from parental supervision. He and his three sisters formed a close-knit and loving unit.

West Downs

In September 1919 when Johnny was eight years old he was sent off to boarding school at West Downs in Winchester as was the custom of the time amongst families of his sort.

By the time he arrived at the school in September 1919, West Downs had already become one of the leading preparatory schools in the country. The school had been started by Lionel Helbert, a scholar of Winchester and Oxford. Helbert's early career had been as a Clerk to the House of Commons but he felt that he had a vocation as a teacher. He worked as a private tutor in London but was encouraged by his patrons to found a school of his own. He searched for suitable premises and identified a building on the edge of Winchester just beyond the barracks and the prison. In 1897 the site became West Downs School.

West Downs was unique because of the way that Helbert conceived of how he would run it. Unlike any other preparatory school in Britain at the time, its founding principle was that it would be a regime based on kindness. Until then, preparatory schools had been notorious as places of brutality where small boys were sent by their fathers to be turned into potential rulers of Britain's vast empire. Such schools were harsh and their inmates loathed them.

West Downs was different. Helbert imaginatively related to the mothers of the boys, not to their fathers, and wrote to each mother every Sunday evening giving them the latest news of their child's progress. After only three years in operation, the school had become the most fashionable in Britain and was bursting at the seams.

The intake of 1919 was typical of its time and a number of the new boys would be of future significance in my father's life – and in my own. Amongst these was Christopher *Kit* Dawnay, who started his career as a stock broker in the City; joined the Coldstream Guards at the outbreak of WWII and became Field Marshall Bernard Montgomery's personal staff officer in the Normandy campaign of 1944. My father looked to *Kit* to find him an appointment on the Staff after he had fought the arduous battles that he knew he would face in Normandy. Kit's son Guy was a friend of mine at the school in the 1950s.

Edward Ford fought the war in the Grenadier Guards before becoming Assistant Private Secretary to HM Queen Elizabeth II. He once saved my life by vouching for my good character when I met my future wife's parents for the first time on a visit to her home at Sandringham in Norfolk.

Edward, who was staying at Sandringham House at the time, confirmed that I must be a good egg if I was the son of Johnnie Fass!

Arthur Hazlerigg was the descendant of one of the four Parliamentary plotters of 1642 about whom King Charles remarked 'I see that the birds have flown'. He had a distinguished career as a gunner in WWII winning the Military Cross in Italy and played cricket for Leicestershire. His daughter Christine married a lifelong friend of mine, Tim Macdowel, the son of a brother officer of my father's in the Royal Berkshire Regiment.

Mark Norman was at Eton with Michael Verey; joined the Hertfordshire Yeomanry in 1939 and later served in the War Cabinet offices, the very centre of Winston Churchill's control of the war effort and a place with which my father was to become familiar as a D-Day planner. After the war he became a banker at Lazards where Kit Dawnay was managing director. In a subsequent generation, my first cousin David, son of Michael Verey, would be Chairman of the firm in his turn.

In the year above (1918) Peter Scott, the son of Captain Falcon Scott was to become a close friend of my father's. Peter used to stay with the Fass family at Inkpen during the holidays. In the following year (1920) my father's first cousin John, the eldest of the Wrightson boys, arrived at the school. The school list was full of names that my father - and later my mother - referred to as friends that included: Allhuson, Astor, Baring, Birchall, Colville, Duckworth, Dugdale, Granville, Holland-Martin, Raikes and Strutt.

West Downs was a happy place to be a schoolboy. The regime was based on the scouting principles of Baden Powell and each boy was placed in a Patrol in which all of its members were expected to look out for one another. My father was in the Owl Patrol (as I was when I joined the school in 1952). Each new boy was allocated a Pater (father) who was responsible for his welfare or 'showing him the ropes' in the first six weeks after his arrival at the school.

In the Scouts my father would have learned useful skills in living outdoors with the Scouts' emphasis on tying knots, lighting fires and signalling messages. This may well have encouraged him in his childhood interest in soldiers and later served him well in the OTC at Rugby School. All the boys had to learn the Scout Promise that included the line that scouts should 'smile and whistle under all difficulties'. This may have helped to re-enforce the sunny nature for which he would later be universally known. My children (and now my grandchildren) grind their teeth and fall back as far as possible as I whistle my way along any street on which I am walking.

My father had a very fine treble voice and sang in the choir in the West Downs chapel that formed the centre of the life of the school community. There was a service in chapel every evening and twice on Sundays. He also sang solo and my mother recalls him telling her of his singing 'Jesu Joy of Man's Desiring' in Chapel during Lent, as I did myself 31 years later.

Rugby

In September 1924, aged 13 and after five years at the school, my father left West Downs and went to Rugby where his father Ernest had been before him. Rugby was a traditional public school made famous in the nineteenth century by its reforming headmaster Dr. Arnold. Arnold had initiated a process that would change the character not only of Rugby but of all the great public schools of England. There would be more emphasis on the intellectual development of the boys and some improvement in the pastoral side of their care. This led to the creation of the house system in which each boy would live in a boarding house, rather than lodging in town, and would have a housemaster who would be responsible for their care and progress. Johnny was in 'FWO's, or F W Odgers Esq. The headmaster at the time was V V Vaughan.

Only two end of term reports of my father's have survived. The first was at the end of the summer term (Trinity) in 1927 when he was 16 years old. He was at a critical time in his career both at school and as a teenager. He was placed 8/29 in the second half of the term's final order and his form master commented 'good. He has made a creditable advance'. However, his housemaster's report suggested that significant change had occurred: 'This has been a capital term in many ways' and the Headmaster's endorsement echoed this feeling: 'I rejoice at this – the beginning of good times'.

It was clearly a pivotal moment in his school career. In the following two years he would have responsibilities and enjoy privileges as he moved from the junior to the senior part of the boarding house and school.

In July 1928 aged 17 and after four years at Rugby, he passed the Oxford and Cambridge Schools Examination Board's school certificate in nine subjects gaining Distinction in English, history and mathematics. By this time he was playing hockey for the school and hockey, rugby and cricket for his house (Kilbracken's) and was awarded house and school colours in these sports. He was also a keen yachtsman and rider on his own 14.2 hands horse named *Bell*.

He had a final year at Rugby beginning in September 1928. At the end of the Lent term in 1929 when he was almost 18, he was placed 2/23 in science but only 24/27 overall in the second half of the term's list. His form master wrote: 'Satis. His absence once a week through military duties, handicaps him'. However, in spite of this comment in his final remarks his form master wrote 'Must keep going in school. He has done capital work in the OTC and elsewhere'. His housemaster wrote: 'I very much appreciate his enthusiasm and his cheerfulness. He is a great help in the house' and the headmaster wrote: 'This has been a really good term. He must aim at getting into the VI (form) proper'.

Enthusiasm and cheerfulness would later become the by-words of his character and career.

From these reports with their references to the OTC it can be inferred that my father pulled his weight in the classroom and in the house and was beginning to develop his military skills. There is no record of the way that he decided on a career in the Army but it is clear from his reports that his interests were more sporting than intellectual so that the next step of a place at a university would have held less attraction for him than that of military training.

He left Rugby in July 1929 and shortly afterwards took the entrance examination for the Royal Military College, Sandhurst. He was awarded a much coveted Prize Cadetship that was worth a proportion of the annual fees and this would have accounted for the telegram that his father sent to him at Foxhill dated 8th August 1929 with the words 'Well done'!

Chapter Three
THE ROYAL MILITARY COLLEGE

The Royal Military College had been founded by forward-looking senior army officers in the mid-18th century as a way to improve the quality of officers entering the British Army. One of these founders, General Gaspar Le Marchant, Wellington's favourite cavalry commander, was my son in law, Rupert Douglas-Pennant's, great-great grandfather. It was at a time when commissions were gained by money purchase and could be held by boys as young as twelve years old whose family were wealthy. However, the idea of a professionally trained body of potential military leaders was increasingly attractive as Britain's overseas territories expanded.

By the time that my father arrived at the College it had become famous for the training of young men to the highest standards of efficiency who would become commissioned officers in the British Army on their graduation or 'passing out'. The RMC was the epitome of smartness, high standards, discipline and tradition. This was an organisation that trained young men to become officers, to lead and, if need be, to die. The cadets would learn discipline, order, skill at arms and the organisation of men and material. In 1929 the Commandant was Major-General Sir Eric Girdwood, an Irishman who had commanded Divisions in France and the Middle East in the 1914-1918 War.

There is no account by my father of his time as a Cadet at the RMC but it is possible to refer to two contemporary accounts that provide a comprehensive description of the experience. The first is David Niven's *The Moon's a Balloon.* Niven had been at Stowe before joining the RMC in 1927. He passed out in July 1929 the year that my father entered. There is a letter written by my father to my mother in October 1940 that records that my father had met Niven in the bar of the Ritz during a night out in London during the blitz 'who he had not seen for ages and who was most friendly'. The second account is from John Masters *Bugles and a Tiger*. Masters arrived from Wellington in 1933 two years after my father left. I have assumed that my father's experience would have been very similar to theirs.

Although my father's official title on arrival at the RMC was Gentleman Cadet John Fass, the cadets had the reputation of being 'not quite officers and not quite gentlemen' (Niven).

The College's eighteen months course was organised in three 'divisions'; junior, intermediate and senior in four Companies, each of six months duration. The junior division was managed by promoted cadets from the senior division.

There were 257 juniors in my father's intake of September 1929 and the early emphasis was on drill as the cadets had to 'pass off the square' after ten weeks. Masters described the event: 'as we were getting ready for parade we saw a group of officers standing negligently in wait for us, gorgeous persons in dark blue frock coats aflutter with broad blue ribbons, and gold brimmed hats, and swords in metal scabbards.' They came from the Guards Depot at Pirbright.

The cadets' hair was shorn like sheep and the pressure to be on time and properly turned out for every drill was intense but it was a 'tough and exhilarating' regime and the cadets were a 'dedicated corps d'elite' (Niven). These first weeks on the square were hard and were punctuated by 'vigorous inspections carried out by the Adjutant and his Drill team whose smartness of turn-out and attention to the highest standards was legendary' (Masters).

The Drill Instructors were drawn exclusively from the Regiments of the Brigade of Guards who were world-famous for their ferocity on the parade ground. My father's two Drill Instructors were from the Grenadier and the Coldstream Guards who 'treated us like mud with no malice or aforethought (Niven). The year before my father joined, there had been an incident of bullying that had reached the national newspapers and the headmaster of Wellington had described the RMC as 'that hell on the hill' (Masters).

It was an extremely tough regime even for a young man who had survived the rigours of his public school. Masters wrote of these early days on the square. 'Many boys have spoken about the violent transition from being a senior boy at school to joining up. From privilege to privation; from demanding respect from their juniors to being run ragged around the parade ground. But at 18, they were 'young, fit and keen' (Masters). 'We drank a great deal, but we were immensely physically fit' (Niven).

Like my father, Masters was a prize cadet of whose performance the instructors took special note: 'They were immediately subject to a form of exquisite torment by their instructing officers who were the crème de la crème of the British Army' (Masters). My father would be appointed an instructor at the RMC in his turn in 1938.

The cadets of the RMC were somewhat isolated behind the College's walls. The General Strike took place in 1926, three years before my father was commissioned, and there was mass unemployment and hunger marches nationally. A cadet was 'a square member of a very square group' (Niven). Casual dress reflected the fashion of the time: 'loud check jackets, baggy trousers and large flat caps at a jaunty angle' (Masters).

As their time at the RMC passed, all cadets settled into the normal pattern of activities that included taking part in sports and representing their Company against other companies and the RMC against other clubs and institutions, for example, those at Oxford and Cambridge. My father played rugby for his Company and hockey for the RMC. As a senior he was awarded a Distinction in the final order for his physical training and drill. Cadets also spent time in the equitation centre which would have been no hardship for my father who was already an accomplished and dedicated horseman.

In the intermediate division it was possible to be made up to cadet-corporal and in the senior division to cadet-sergeant. My father was one of four cadet-sergeants in his Company as a senior.

Insinuated into the mind of each cadet from the very beginning of their time at the RMC was the matter of the Regiment or Corps that they wished to join after passing out and being commissioned as officers. In the days of the pre-war British Army this was about a number of factors that included 'connection', choices, aptitude and necessity, the latter usually related to 'means' or money.

Another important factor would be their place in the final 'list'. For example, the Regiments of the Indian Amy would take only those who were placed high on it.

The cadets spent much mental anguish on this subject and the issue became a particularly problematic one for my father.

It had been clear from the beginning that the Regiment of his first choice would the Coldstream Guards of his family's Neame connection. At the RMC he had seen the way that the officers and NCOs of the Brigade of Guards had the smartest turn-out and occupied the key positions in its hierarchy. For example, the Adjutant was always drawn from the Brigade. Masters describes the Adjutant of his time, a Coldstreamer, as 'beautiful beyond belief with his dark blue hat, red face, glassy boots and golden spurs who strode slowly among our scurrying squads, communing in silent scorn with some Coldstream deity who hovered a hundred feet up in the air in front of him.'

However, when his father asked him which regiment he wanted to go for and my father replied "the Coldstream", there was an immediate froideur. My grandfather told my father that he would not be able to survive on his pay as a junior officer and that the Regiment would be much too expensive for Ernest to finance. To be fair, the regiments of the Brigade of Guards served most of their time in London and it would be an expensive place for a young officer to live with little private income. As a writer commented:

"Such regiments maintained their social exclusivity by a system of punitively high mess bills and expenses, making it impossible for an officer without independent means to pay his way" (Allport).

My father's second choice - subject always, of course, to the final list! - would be to join the 5th Royal Inniskilling Dragoon Guards known as *The Skins*, a first class cavalry regiment in which a number of his friends at the RMC were hoping to serve. In this Regiment he could further develop his passion for riding as all its young officers were expected to be mounted; to follow the hunt; to ride in steeplechases and to compete at point-to-point races in winter and play polo in the summer - Ideal!

When my father tried this one on he got the same response from his father, Ernest: Horses at stables were expensive and his father was not going to pay for them!

At this point - and probably close to despair - the young man asked his father for advice: What would be an acceptable Regiment to his father for him to join? He received the inauspicious response which was that he could join his local County Regiment, the Royal Berkshire Regiment. The Colonel of the Regiment was Major General F F Ready, Quartermaster General to the Forces who was married to a distant Cotterill cousin of his mother Winnie. The General was known to Ernest in Whitehall and - it was implied - his father could fix it for his son.

And so it was arranged. My father was not able to join the Regiment of his choice and it took him another eight years in the army and the threat of a second world war for him to realise his ambition to serve as one of the elite of the Brigade of Guards.

However, he was not alone. Niven had suffered the same agonies two years earlier.

Niven's mother had left no stone unturned in her attempts to get her son into the Argyll and Sutherland Highlanders, a regiment that both she and her son thought of as a glamorous outfit. His father had been killed at Gallipoli serving with the Berkshire Yeomanry. She pulled every string that included meetings not only with the Colonel of the Regiment, The Maclean of Loch Buie, but also with its Royal Honorary Colonel, Princess Louise, sister of King George V. A few weeks before the end of his final term, by now a cadet in the senior division and an under-officer in his Company, Niven completed the form issued by the War Office that asked: 'Name in order of preference three regiments into which you desire to be commissioned'. Niven wrote as follows:

> 'The Argyll and Sutherland Highlanders
> The Black Watch
> *Anything but* the Highland Light Infantry'

Niven wrote subsequently: 'somebody at the War Office was funnier than I was and I was promptly commissioned into the HLI!'

In the final list that took into account the total marks awarded to my father throughout his eighteen months at the RMC, he performed exceptionally well and was placed fourth on the list out of 172 graduating cadets who completed the course. He had risen 25 places from his original position as a Prize Cadet at entry in 1929 and as a result he was awarded a further Army bursary worth £50 per year for the next five years. His total marks were 5391/6600 or 82% overall with 545/600 or 91% from his Company Commander.

At the end of January 1931 my father received the following from the War Office addressed to:

J.E. Fass
Second Lieutenant
Land Forces
The Royal Berkshire Regiment
(Princess Charlotte of Wales's)
30.1.1931

George the Fifth by the Grace of God of Great Britain, Ireland and the British Dominions beyond the Seas, King, Defender of the Faith, Emperor of India, etc.

To Our Trusty and well beloved *John Ernest Fass* Greetings

We reposing especial Trust and Confidence in your Loyalty, Courage and good Conduct. Do by these Presents Constitute and Appoint you to be an Officer in Our Land Forces from the *twenty-ninth* day of *January* 19*31*. You are therefore carefully and diligently to discharge your Duty as such in the rank of *Second Lieutenant* or in such other

Rank as We may from time to time hereafter be pleased to
promote or appoint you to, of which a notification will
be made in the London Gazette, or in such other manner as
may for the time being be prescribed by Us in Council,
and you are in such manner and on such occasions as may
be prescribed by Us to exercise and well discipline Arms
both the inferior Officers and Men serving under you and
use your best endeavours to keep them in good Order and
Discipline.
And We do hereby Command them to Obey you as their
superior Officer; and you to observe and follow such
Orders and Directions as from time to time you shall
receive from Us. Or any your superior Officer, according
to the Rules and Discipline of War, in pursuance of the
Trust hereby reposed in you.

Given at Our Court, at Saint James. the *twenty-sixth* Day
of *January,* 1931, in the *twenty-first* Year of Our Reign.

John Ernest Fass By His Majesty's Command
Second Lieutenant

He had received his Commission and would join his Regiment.

The final and prescient words about my father's time at the RMC should
go to Niven and Masters.

> 'A heartbreakingly high percentage (of cadets) were destined in a
> little more than ten year's time to meet their deaths on the beaches,
> deserts and hillsides of World War II. This was the vintage of soldiers
> that suffered most heavily when the holocaust came' (Niven).

and

> 'He was joining an army in which in the passing of the years he
> would reach maturity as a senior officer at a time when civilisation
> would need him. He would lead men and hold high responsibility
> in the greatest conflict ever fought. It was as a result of this (RMC)
> experience that he was ready to take his place as a leader in the
> greatest volunteer army that the world has ever seen' (Masters).

Chapter Four
THE REGIMENT

Between February and September 1931 my father was first on graduation leave and then took the young officers 'Qualifying Course' at the School of Musketry at Hythe in Kent. There is a group photograph of the course members who would have been newly graduated young officers like himself and all well known to him from the RMC. He is one of five seated in the front row out of forty on the course. Perhaps this was because he was one of those who had passed out with the first "Distinguished" award on his military record. Finally, on the 20ᵗʰ October he was posted to the Second Battalion, The Royal Berkshire Regiment (Princess Charlotte of Wales's).

History and tradition

Both my father and Niven had already experienced something of the way that the British Army was structured in their attempts to join the regiments of their choice. First came the Brigade of Guards, next the cavalry and lastly the regiments of the Infantry of the Line. The title of the regiment that my father joined the *Second Battalion, The Royal Berkshire Regiment (Princess Charlotte of Wales's)* was typical of its kind. It had been formed originally in 1756 in the Seven Years War as the 66ᵗʰ Regiment of Foot and had been stationed in the West Indies, Canada, Ceylon and India. Its 2ⁿᵈ Battalion had fought with Wellington in the Peninsular and had distinguished itself in all of the great battles of that long campaign including the crossing of the Douro and at Talavera (1809), Busaco (1810), Albuera (1811) - at which it had suffered heavy losses due to Wellington's absence from the battlefield – at Vittoria (1813) and at the Nivelle and the Nive (1813). In 1816 the Regiment had guarded the exiled Emperor Bonaparte on St Helena after his defeat at Waterloo until his death in 1821.

In 1880 the Regiment was ordered to Afghanistan. The British had invaded a year earlier after the murder of its imperial envoy and his escort. The country appeared to be pacified and the 66th who had marched up from India were expected to act as a garrison only and not to meet opposition. However, the brother of the deposed Emir led a counter-attack and on the 27th July, the 66th, as part of a mixed force of Indian and British infantry, was sent to Maiwand to prevent their advance.

A combination of poor general-ship, the uneven ground and vastly superior enemy numbers all worked against the smaller British and Indian force and by mid-afternoon of the 27th, most of the Indian soldiers were dead or had fled and of the 66th there were few survivors. The Regiment had fought valiantly throughout the day but it was finally overwhelmed and its last stand was made in an orchard by two officers and nine men who continued to fire steadily. Only when the last man was shot down did the Ghazis swarm amongst them. Of the 19 officers and 427 other ranks who had gone into battle, 10 officers and 275 men had been killed. It is believed that the author Arthur Conon Doyle based his fictional character Dr. Watson, Sherlock Holmes' assistant, on the 66th's medical officer who was portrayed as having served with the Regiment in the campaign.

When news of the defeat reached Victorian England, the whole population went wild with grief at the brave stand of the *Last Eleven* of the 66th and mawkish patriotic sentiment, typical of the time, washed over the whole country. The Commander in Chief, India had written home:

'History does not afford any grander or finer instance of gallantry and devotion to Queen and Country than that displayed by the 66th Regiment on the 27th July 1880.' (Myatt)

On their return to England the 'Die Hard' heroes of Albuera and the Peninsular were received by Queen Victoria at Osborne on the Isle of Wight where Her Majesty presented them with new Colours but the battle of Maiwand was to be their last as soldiers of the old 66th. The

Colours presented on that day were the same stand that my father would carry on parade more than 50 years later.

As the British Empire had expanded throughout the 19th century, the need for troops to pacify and police its newly acquired territories became a pressing issue for successive governments and in 1881 the Secretary of State for War, Edward Cardwell, proposed a new organisation for the Army as a way to improve its recruiting.

Each existing regiment would be grouped with another and would have two battalions of which one would be posted overseas and the other stationed in the home country at any one time. Each of these new regiments would have a home depot and be affiliated to a locality. As a result of these changes the 'Old 66th' was amalgamated with the 49th Regiment of Foot and became its *Second Battalion.*
The new regiment's local affiliation would be to the County of Berkshire, with which the 66th had enjoyed a previous association, and its Depot would be located at the newly built Brock Barracks in Reading.

The Regiment's new First Battalion, formerly the 49th, had impressed King George III when he had inspected it at Weymouth in 1816 on its return from Canada after the Battle of Queenstown and had appointed his granddaughter, Princess Charlotte of Wales as its colonel, hence its name. Between 1854 - 1857, the 49th had fought in the Crimea at the battles of Alma, Inkerman and Balaclava and in the Opium Wars of 1839 before being joined with the 66th to form The Berkshire Regiment (Princess Charlotte of Wales's) in 1881.

In 1885 the new regiment was appointed a Royal Regiment for the action of its First Battalion at the battle of Tofrek in the Sudan:

'Her Majesty has been graciously pleased, in recognition of the gallant conduct of Princess Charlotte of Wales's (Berkshire Regiment) in the action at Tofrek, to approve of the Regiment being in future designated Princess Charlotte of Wales's Royal Berkshire Regiment'. (Myatt)

The Regiment took the China Dragon of the 49th as its emblem with the word *China* below for its badges and buttons and retained the Stag and Oak Tree of the 66th – marking its association with Berkshire - for its helmets and other accoutrements.

One benefit of the Cardwell reforms was that the new regular Regiment could now be linked to existing local Militia and Volunteer forces in the County. These were formed into Territorial units which were to play a prominent part in the first half of the 20th century when the Regiment fought in the second South African, or Boer War, and in the 1914-1918 Great War. The Great War was to involve the Regiment in military operations of a scale and intensity previously unknown and over its five years the Regiment fought in every major campaign including Mons and First Ypres (1914), Loos and Neuve Chapelle (1915) and at the Somme (1916) where it lost twenty officers and 437 soldiers. Fifty-five new Battle Honours were won and 6688 of all ranks of the Regiment died winning them.

In the Second World War the Regiment also fought with distinction in France, the Far East and in Western Europe. A Company Commander of the Second Battalion wrote later of his experience:

> 'It was the regimental tradition that kept us going when times were hard. The knowledge that throughout the ages – at Maiwand, at Tofrek in Eygpt in 1885, at Boulon Wood in France in 1917 and at Kohima in 1944 – the Regiment had, before the eyes of the world, fought according to the highest traditions of the service, both in victory and in defeat, was our foundation and inspiration.' (Hill)

In 1967 as a result of the reorganisation of the volunteer forces, the Berkshire Yeomanry, in which I served, was suspended for a brief period and I was re-badged as a Royal Berkshire Territorial under the Colonelcy of my uncle, Lt.-Col. Philip Verey who had joined the Regiment as a Territorial in the 1930s and had fought in it throughout the Second World War.

Young Officer
By the time that my father joined the Second Battalion in 1931 the massive increase in the armed services that had been needed to fight and

win the Great War were in the past and the British Army was in a parlous state. The country had been financially broken by the costs of the War in men and materiel, the post-war economic depression that followed and the Financial Crash of 1929. Savings had to be made in every budget and sixteen officers of the Regiment had been made redundant at the time of the *Geddes Axe* in 1921.

The Government introduced the *Ten year rule* which assumed that there would be no general war for 10 years on a rolling basis with the result that no investment was made in the Army's arms or equipment throughout the period and it became a diminished and disabled institution. Horsed cavalry and artillery were still in use and the development of armoured fighting vehicles was minimal. On manoeuvres red flags were waved to represent the opposing forces and rattles were spun to simulate machine gun fire. Before the outbreak of World War II, the Army was a gendarmerie that provided security for Great Britain's empire and was not a war-fighting machine.

It is testament to the strength and endurance of the regimental system and of the loyalty and efficiency of the British Army's soldiers, officers and staff that this reduced cadre of professionals sustained itself throughout this long period of neglect. The Army would not be taken seriously again until after Hitler's rise to power in 1933 and the Munich crisis of 1938 by which time it was almost too late.

My father's early service was set in this bleak era for the British Army but it was still able to offer an active and enjoyable life for a certain type of young man. In time, many of these men would provide the foundation for the mass mobilisation that would be needed when the Second World War broke out in 1939. It was inevitable, therefore, that in the early years of the war, the main task of many of those who had served in the pre-war army would be to assemble and train a new generation of volunteers and this would be one of my father's principal wartime activities.

The arrival of a newly commissioned officer into his regiment could be daunting. My father may have done well at the Royal Military College but that would have been a very different experience to being made responsible for a group of time-served soldiers drawn from the

County and elsewhere in Britain some of whom with experience of war-fighting.

Both Niven and Masters commented on their first meeting with their platoons:

'Sergeant Innes was waiting for me. "I'll take you to the barrack room so you can see your platoon". So this was it – the moment of truth! At last I was about to come face to face with the professionals who would be under my command. This was the crunch. In a strange mood of exaltation, I marched confidently alongside Sergeant Innes. Outside a barrack room door, excitedly marked *No 3 Platoon,* Sergeant Innes stopped – then flung it open. A stentorian bellow rent the air: "Stand by your beds!" A sound of scuffling feet came from within. After that silence. "No. 3 Platoon ready for your inspection, Sir". Proudly, I passed him to confront, for the first time, my long-awaited charges. Seven rather crestfallen soldiers in various stages of undress stood waiting for me beside their beds.'

Back at the Company office the Company Sergeant Major gently explained that for a young officer still in his teens, trained to the hilt, and pumped full of ambition and enthusiasm to find himself in a home service battalion of very diminished strength fulfilling garrison duties while completing its own training programme and at the same time as being constantly drained of its best men, the result was almost inevitable - deadening frustration' (Niven).

and

'I had stood helplessly facing my first command, overcome with self-consciousness, while the amazed soldiers laughed openly at me. I had found that I could not open my mouth to give an order, not even "Dismiss". The soldiers said loudly to one another "Cor, look at 'im", and "E's a funny-looking little officer inee?". Sergeant Broadhurst snapped at them until they, secretly as embarrassed as I, fell silent. I pulled myself together at last, with an enormous effort of will, and gave the command "Attention". (Masters).

There was one further ritual that a newly commissioned young officer had to go through which was that of being *dined in* by their regiment; that is being formally introduced into the regimental family. This usually happened within the first six weeks of joining at a special dinner night arranged in the Officer's Mess.

Masters refers to this experience in the Ghurkas:

'A guest night was approaching, at which I would be ceremoniously *dined into* the regiment. Days ahead I started to worry over the details of my dress and appearance. On the night my shirt was as stiff and white as it could be, my black tie beautifully tied and my mess Wellingtons polished like mirrors. After walking into the anteroom, I checked at attention with proper carefully rehearsed carelessness, and said "Good evening, Sir," to the senior officer present..... who replied "Well, this is the last time you'll be a regimental guest until you get married, so make the best of it" (Masters).

as does the regimental historian of the Berkshires:

'The Commanding Officer was preceded from the ante-room into the dining room by a drummer in full dress, with sticks softly rustling on the drum on which it was reputed that the Convention of Cintra was signed in 1802. The gentle sound was just audible above the band playing "The Roast Beef of Old England", and continued until a second drummer faced him from across the table, denoting that the last dining officer was present. A click of sticks, and they withdrew into the shadows, leaving the room, with its gleaming silver, the bowls of roses, the snuff boxes and cigar cutters, the carefully selected trophies and the massive centrepiece, shining against a dark polished table in the soft light of the candelabra, while the staff in livery began to serve the meal. And then before the toast of "The King", still came the agonising moment when the long white strips of tablecloth, twenty feet or more, were removed, each with a straight undeviating pull' (Blight).

The men of the Regiment were drawn not only from across the County of Berkshire but also from London (Hackney) and the North (Durham) in order to make up their numbers at a time of limited recruiting. The farm boys from the west of the County tended to be slower on the uptake but utterly reliable and good with the troop horses of the Battalion. The men of Reading and the larger towns were faster to pick up new ideas and gadgets when these were introduced. Both in their own ways made good soldiers and, when promoted, reliable NCOs (Non Commissioned Officers) who led the four sections of each Platoon and used its specialist weapons. The Regiment's nickname in the rest of the British Army was 'The Biscuit Boys' in recognition of their base at Reading, the home of Huntley & Palmers, biscuit manufacturers.

Because of both its historic and county connection with the Royal Family, the Regiment prided itself on its smartness of turn-out and overall competence. As the local Regiment it provided the demonstration platoons for the RMC when needed and the gentleman cadets spent time at its Depot in Reading familiarising themselves with Army life. The Dragon Club tent provided hospitality each year at Royal Ascot and the Regiment's annual cricketing week in July played host to a variety of military and sporting clubs from all over the South East of England. On manoeuvres it was held in high esteem as a *marching regiment* and at leisure its officers were expected to ride out with the Garth and South Berks Hunts and participate in regimental and other local point-to-point meetings.

My father's arrival at the Second Battalion coincided with its move from Aldershot to Folkestone where he met and commanded his first Platoon of Berkshiremen. The barracks were set on the top of the cliffs above the harbour and were bleak. Soon, however, with much effort, the place was made more habitable and the annual round of an infantry battalion's life was put in progress. The Battalion numbered some 400 soldiers which was approximately half its nominal strength so my father's Platoon probably had no more than twenty men. This was partly because of poor recruiting, partly the effects of cuts in manpower demanded by the Treasury and partly because under the old Cardwell system that had been restored at the end of WWI, the home service battalion providing reinforcements for the battalion serving overseas to bring it up to full strength, in this case to the First Battalion serving in India.

Young officers spent their days supervising their men on the rifle ranges, inspecting feet and equipment and organising sports of every kind. Masters described his early experience with his platoon:

'The Regiment laboured to teach me the basic techniques of my profession and some of the intangibles which, they seemed to believe, held men together in times of stress, whatever men's colour or creed. I played football, ran cross-country with my platoon. I inspected its smelly feet and noisome socks and sat up and listened to its involved stories of domestic betrayal.

I congratulated it, admonished it, put it under arrest, and admired its snapshots...I spent weeks on the rifle range, supervising the training of soldiers in marksmanship. I sat for hours in Quartermasters stores, counting ammunition and entering rows of figures in ledgers' (Masters).

The Berkshires had a prominent boxing team that fought in contests all along the South Coast and the most popular sporting activity for officers was riding, my father's favourite recreation. He hunted with the East Kent hounds and the Shorncliffe Draghounds as well as taking part in local point-to-points. As a noted rider my father took his share of the responsibility for mounted activities and stabling and is shown in a photograph with his team of soldiers preparing for an equestrian event, probably to serve as the arena party for the Shorncliffe Garrison's horse show and military display, that was held each year in July. In 1932 he attended the Army's Veterinary Course in Aldershot where he developed further his riding and horse management skills. At the end of the course, as for musketry, he was again awarded "Distinguished".

There is also evidence that he did not neglect his social life. There were both regimental and civil social occasions and by all accounts he was an attractive escort. It was at this time that he probably embarked on the first of a number of youthful entanglements with women who he liked to call his *lovelies*. Forty years later I recall being introduced to an older woman at a party who was one of three daughters of a local landowner. When she heard my name she asked: "Are you related to *Johnny* Fass?"

and when I confirmed that I was his son, she blushed to the roots of her hair!

At the beginning of 1934 my father was sent on another course, the Regimental Signalling Instructors Course at Catterick in Yorkshire that lasted for three months. This was a fortuitous appointment because it was close to Neasham Hall, the home of his first cousin and best friend Peter Wrightson with whom he spent most of his spare time whilst on the course. It was a riotous household organised around the four Wrightson boys and there was plenty of opportunity for fun and games at weekends as well as shooting. Whenever possible throughout the course he hunted with the Zetland hounds and was mounted by the Marquess from his seat at Aske in North Yorkshire.

It was written of the Zetland Hunt at the time:

> 'After the Great War a new era dawned for the hunt seeing that Catterick has now become established as a large military camp and from this mobile source of supply there flows a continuous stream of keen riding officers, many of whom go exceedingly well across country. Thus our personnel is reinforced with a group of younger men, the charm of whose gaiety and courage affects the hunt company in more ways than one.' (Stewart)

He renewed boyhood friendships out hunting that included the Fife, Pease, Straker and Vaux families and hunted over country with which he was familiar from Neasham including Beverly Woods, Cliffe, Middleton Tyas, Rockerby and West Auckland. These connections and places would also play a part in his later career when he was appointed a Brigade Major and stationed in Northumberland in May 1941.

In more ways than one may well be a reference to my father because he became so close to one of the Marquess's daughters that they apparently got unofficially engaged! He was 23 and she was just 20 so that any idea of marriage was quite out of the question. In those days young officers were required to have completed at least eight years of service before getting married and then were only allowed to do so with the permission of their commanding officer. This issue of marriage would become a serious problem when he and my mother wished to get married three years later.

On the back of a photograph that his Northern *lovely* sent to him when he had returned to the Battalion at the end of the course in April were written the words: "As I was when you knew me" and "This will fade away quite soon as it is a proof but no doubt you will have forgotten me before then". Someone's heart had been broken! In the group photograph taken at the end of the course he is shown in the front row this time seated next to HRH the Duke of Gloucester, third son of King George V and an officer of the Scots Guards. At the end of the course he was once again awarded "Distinguished".

In the summer of 1934 the battalion was ordered overseas and its numbers were made up by drafts from the First Battalion which was returning from India to occupy the same barracks at Shorncliffe. Shortly before embarkation he was appointed Assistant Adjutant to help with all the extra work that this entailed and was promoted to Lieutenant. One rite of passage had been his attendance at a Royal Levee which meant being presented to King George V at Buckingham Palace. Niven described his experience at a similar event:

> 'Inside St James's Palace was most impressive. Two large ante-rooms filled with several young officers from all branches of the three services. It was a blaze of colour – Highlanders, Hussars, Greenjackets, Gentlemen at Arms, Indian cavalry officer in turbans, Ghurkhas and Maharajas. There was a suppressed bonhomie in the first ante-room as many old friends were recognised, some from Sandhurst. The second ante-room into which we were later directed was quiet and one sensed a certain nervousness. It took about two hours to percolate through the two ante-rooms and into the Throne Room where we were to pay our respects to King George V. (Niven)

Hence my father's remark in a letter he wrote to his mother:

> 'The Levee was quite one of the worst functions I have ever attended.

One stood about in a very tight uniform for hours and hours in an awful squash of people.'

His Platoon now numbered thirty four men including seven NCOs which brought it up to its full fighting strength.

These first three years of service had affirmed my father in his choice of career. He was now a useful member of the Regiment and had learned his basic soldiering skills at which he had excelled. He had participated in every sporting and riding opportunity that was offered to him and he had experienced his first command, much of it in the training of soldiers.

Masters described this introduction to life in his Ghurka Regiment as:

'I realized that the Regiment without seeming to take any trouble over it, was beginning to train me on four parallel lines – one of the body, one of the brain, one of the character and one of the spirit. The first was easy enough. Every year we marched about 1500 miles... at the same time the Regiment imparted to me some of its many skills and my brain was acquiring army techniques. Simultaneously I saw that these skills are directed by the character, and without that have no purpose. The Regiment did nothing overt to improve my character, it left it to me, giving me only good and bad examples and leaving me to draw my own conclusions. And I saw that ability was not really very important. It was for the conscientious, thoughtful, brave, and, above all, straightforward man that people gave their best.

The fourth and greatest gift was also left lying about on the ground, on or off parade – for me to treasure if I had the capacity. This was the spirit of the Regiment... the spirit of the Regiment took little heed of efficiency, discipline or loyalty. It had been built up by generations of men. It was for this spirit that we drilled together, got drunk together, hunted, danced, played, killed and saved life together. It was from this spirit that no man was alone, neither on the field of battle, which is a lonely place, nor in the chasm of death, nor in the dark places of life' (Masters).

My father was now about to put all of this to good effect as he packed his trunks to embark on active service although he was annoyed that at the same time that he was leaving for the Middle East his parents were returning from their stay in the Sudan and wrote to his mother 'it's awful this leaving England business – it's such a confounded nuisance for a start and also I'm not looking forward to it one bit'.

Before my father left England, an event had taken place in the late spring of 1934 that was to shape the remainder of his life. He had attended the South Berks Hunt point-to-point meeting in the company of a number of brother officers one of whom was Philip Verey, who was serving in the Regiment's 4th/6th Territorial Battalion. In the course of the day Philip had introduced my father to his sister Elizabeth. Three years later they were to marry.

Left to right: Margaret (Peggy), Aunt Gertrude (Neame?) , Mary-Maria, JEF (aged 7) and Susan (at foot).

Holidays at Hartland Bay. Left to right: Maria, Susan, JEF and Ernest.

JEF with family dogs.

JEF fishing.

JEF practising for his Scout semaphore badge at West Downs.

JEF April 1928 at Rugby, aged 17.

JEF at Rugby.

JEF on Bell summer 1929 leaving Rugby, aged 18.

The Royal Berkshire Regiment
(Princess Charlotte of Wales's).
1743-1959.

Young officer, Sir John Moore
Barracks, Shorncliffe (1931).

Arena Party, Shorncliffe Military Garrison Horse Show (1933)
Beloved dog 'Dinty' at foot.

Royal Levee at Buckingham Palace,..... 'quite one of the worst functions I have ever attended'. (1934).

During the long Regimental
Signalling Instructors course,
Catterick.
From left to right:
Peter Wrightson, JEF &
Bill Curling at Neasham.
(March 1934)

arking about in his best
unday suit.
atterick. (March 1934)

After lunch walk.
Fifth from left Peter
Wrightson, sixth from left
the lovely', far right JEF.
(March 1934)

'The quality of the Band was particularly remarked upon.......'
(Palestine 1934-1936).

The Royal Berkshire Regiment
Other Ranks Cap Badge

Armistice Day parade, Mount Scopus, British Military Cemetery, Jerusalem, 1934.

n the Polo ground
alestine (1935)

Caption reads: 'Lt. Fass
demonstrating primitive field
kitchen'.

isiting the Navy at Alexandria.

'The standard of turnout was very high....
Palestine 1935

'Berks Adjutant wed in London – County families distinguished guests.'
(Reading Mercury). St Paul's Knightsbridge, 3rd June 1937

Chapter Five
ACTIVE SERVICE

Trooping took place in the autumn months in order to avoid the excruciating heat of the sea route to the East and on the 7th September 1934 the Battalion left its barracks to go down to the Port of Dover. My father described the journey in a letter to his mother:

'Well we had a pretty grim sort of journey down to the boat. Woke up at 1.30am and crept out of barracks at 4.20am and then down to the station in the pitch darkness and off by 5.25am. Hundreds of wives and children to see us off (it was to be an unaccompanied tour). Well then we got down to the boat a thing of about 9000 tons all white with a blue line and yellow funnel. She's pretty old and really rather badly fitted up.'

The Battalion boarded the transport HMT Neuralia bound for its destination, the Port of Haifa in Palestine. On board was a mixed contingent of 1437 soldiers and 80 families of which the Royal Berkshires formed a part. The regimental historian described the scene:

'Many (friends) arrived at Southampton where the battalion thought to embark for eighteen years abroad...........the band under its new master played Auld Land Syne and as the transport drew out into the stream the mournful notes of 'Johnny Fass's hunting horn sounded G-o-n-e-a-w-a-y – G-o-n-e a-w-a-y!' (Blight)

My father wrote to his mother:

'Thousands of people came down to see us off; all the old stiffs from the Regiment. I didn't mind the actual going out although I should have hated you to have been there. You gaze at the dock for hours without being able to talk. Actually I'd got my hunting horn so I made the day hideous with that playing the "Gone away"'.

The voyage on the crowded troopship was to take twelve days and put in at Gibraltar and Malta, where my father aimed to meet up with his sister Maria whose husband Brian was serving with the Mediterranean Fleet and with his sister Susan who was visiting them at the time. He described conditions on board:

'The troops live in absolute squalor all herded together between decks like convicts – they sleep in hammocks by night. I share a tiny cabin, there simply isn't room to swing the smallest kitten with two other people. Actually it's grand we have already broken most of it up and bells ring and infuriated women complain to the steward that we make too much noise. There is nothing to do and nowhere to do it. Actually the trouble is there is simply nowhere one can make a NOISE. The whole place is full of antique Majors and Colonels and the most awful collection of womenfolk I have ever seen in all my life.'

On the 19th September they arrived at the Port of Haifa on the coast of Palestine.

The strategic situation

The presence of British influence and of its forces in the Middle East was designed to fulfil three related roles. First, His Majesty's Government had interests in the Mediterranean sea that stretched from Gibraltar in the West to Alexandria in the East and these relied on the activities of the Royal Navy and its fleet based in Malta. My father's sister, Maria, was married to Brian Logan who was stationed with the Mediterranean Fleet on the island. Second, it was imperative to keep the Suez Canal open to provide the link to Great Britain's territories in India and the Far East and its defence was the responsibility of the Army. My father's third and final posting was in the Canal Zone. Third, Great Britain relied increasingly on the Persian oilfields to power the turbines of its Navy and of its industries at home and the protection of these was provided by the Royal Air Force. My father flew on reconnaissance and training flights with the RAF in this area. Finally, and a specifically Army responsibility, a number of the territories liberated from the Turks at the end of the First World War had been made the responsibility of Great Britain in a Mandate issued by the League of Nations. Palestine was one of these countries and its occupation was to cause its protector no end of trouble. My father's first posting was to Jerusalem.

Palestine had been taken from the Turks as a consequence of Allenby's desert campaign that had ended with his victorious army entering Jerusalem in December 1917.

However, in the division of the spoils of the Ottoman Empire, Britain had accepted something of a poisoned chalice as Palestine had long been an area of conflict for three main reasons. First, from the late 19th century onwards, pressure had been placed on western governments for the foundation of a homeland in Palestine for Jews expelled from the lands of the Russian Empire and its satellites. By 1914 c. 85,000 Jews, mainly from Eastern Europe, had settled in Palestine and their presence had begun to be an aggravation to the indigenous Arab population.

Second, throughout the early years of the First World War, His Majesty's Government had not only given a sympathetic ear to the idea of further Jewish settlement in Palestine but in November 1917 had also formally indicated its future policy in the so-called Balfour Declaration which suggested that 'HMG views with favour the establishment in Palestine of a national home for the Jewish people'.

Third, whilst the Declaration also stated that 'nothing shall be done which may prejudice the civil and religious rights of existing non Jewish communities in Palestine', the damage had already been done. In 1915 the British Foreign Office, in a secret arrangement with their French allies made by Sir Mark Sykes for the British and Georges Picot for the French, had agreed that when the war was over Palestine would be too important a place to leave to the Arabs and their desert allies alone. The Sykes-Picot Pact confirmed that in spite of Arab expectations of freedom promoted amongst others by T E Lawrence, who had led their irregular forces in the war, France and Great Britain would oversee the territories of Syria, the Lebanon and Palestine and rule over their mixed populations.

The Arab Revolt

Whilst an uneasy peace punctuated by sporadic outbreaks of violence had reigned throughout the 1920s, by the beginning of the 1930s the tensions between the two main communities had risen to boiling point. By 1935 total Jewish immigration was at 247,000 and in April 1936 the Arab population rose in revolt against the British partly because of this increase and partly because of real and imagined injustices towards the Arab community of both social and economic origin. When the Battalion arrived in late 1934 both Arabs and Jews were busy consolidating their positions and organising themselves for what both sides regarded as an inevitable conflict.

Since the end of the First World War there had always been a British Army presence in Palestine of at least two infantry battalions of which the 2nd Battalion would be one. The Battalion's duties would be a combination of 'showing the flag' on ceremonial duties in and around the important historic and strategic centre of Jerusalem and of 'maintaining the King's peace' on field exercises and security operations throughout the area in the face of potential and actual civil unrest, the latter as and when it should occur. As my father's service in the Middle East went on, a number of other factors became critical to the security situation that included Mussolini's invasion of Abyssinia in October 1935. As a result my father was first stationed at Jerusalem in Palestine, next at Alexandria in Egypt and finally at Moascar in the Canal Zone, also in Egypt.

Jerusalem

Between disembarkation on the 20th September 1934 and the 4th December 1935, a period of 15 months, the Battalion was stationed in Talavera Barracks in Jerusalem set on a hill above the city's railway station. Whilst the accommodation and facilities were somewhat primitive, the Battalion quickly settled into its role.

Training at both battalion level and with other military detachments was organised that included working with the RAF, the civil police and the

Transjordan Frontier Force. These exercises involved the use of lorries, camels and mule trains and were designed to prepare the Battalion for trouble should it occur. Sporting activities, as usual, took up much of the spare time of both officers and men and cricket, football and athletic matches were arranged against other units in the area. Officers hunted with the Ramleh Vale hounds, played polo and took part in mounted sports and race meetings.

Ceremonial also played a significant part in the Battalion's duties as it provided guards of honour for visiting dignitaries and at other important events that included the annual Armistice Day service and parade held at the British military cemetery at Mount Scopus, trooping the Battalion's Colours on HM the King's official birthday in June and providing the Guard of Honour for a visit by the King of Sweden to Jerusalem. The standard of drill and turnout of the Battalion was very high on these occasions and the quality of its band was particularly remarked upon. The Band possessed eight side drums, four tenor drums, a bass drum, two sets of cymbals and twenty flutes and piccolos. The drum sticks were ebony and silver, the tenor drummers wore panther skins and the bass drummer was dressed in a tiger skin.

There was also occasional enjoyment to be had. A holiday week in honour of the battle of Maiwand was organised that included a donkey fair, a carnival and bathing and boating at the seaside at Jaffa on the coast as well as tours of the Holy Places took place.

My father's letters home to his mother in England reflect the life of a young officer on active service with his Regiment: sometimes exciting and enjoyable but more often than not routine and frustrating. These letters describe the way that my father spent his time which was filled with a combination of military, social, sporting and sightseeing activities as well as the inevitable ennui of an overseas posting.

In one of the first letters to his mother he wrote:

'I don't like this place. The whole trouble is that there is literally *nothing* to do and the place is impossible for riding. Actually the country interests me a bit more and I am beginning to get used to the miles and miles of beastly brown hills. I haven't yet seen any sights and don't know when I'm going to start but must begin sometime or other or otherwise one will become like the proverbial Londoner who doesn't know the way to Westminster Abbey. I had my first game of Polo on Sunday and then played again on Wednesday and hope to play again tomorrow. It was great fun I thought but simply didn't compare with hunting or racing. I don't think I should ever get completely mad about it. It just hasn't got the same thrill about it at all.'

In the course of his two years of service in the Middle East he held a number of posts in the Battalion. These included commanding HQ Company where he was responsible for the Battalion's signallers and also, later on, for its transport. He served as a Platoon Commander in A Company. He was appointed Assistant Adjutant for the move from Jerusalem to Alexandria by train and later was acting Adjutant in Moascar. There was also talk in Moascar of him being made Staff Captain to the Brigade Major of the Canal Brigade under Galloway. These various appointments showed his early promise.

In all his correspondence during his two years of service overseas there was not one military exercise for which my father had much enthusiasm. They were almost always "frightful", "pointless" or "tiresome". He was often tired and either soaking wet, too hot or too cold. On one occasion he and his fellow officers managed to set their tent on fire and as a result he lost his campaign cot and other articles of equipment but managed to save his dinner jacket and his best brown boots. A letter describes one of many military exercises that were held at Platoon, Company and Battalion level:

'We pottered out on Battalion training which was quite awful from start to finish – We started out in a sand storm and after a futile day spent the night under a wall in torrential rain so much so that next morning the rest of the scheme was cancelled and we all hurried back to barracks.'

and on another occasion:

'We sallied forth into the country for Battalion training which was quite appalling and made me wonder why I'd ever considered the army as a career. We started in a sandstorm with a howling gale blowing that night it rained good and hard and everything was absolutely soaked so by the grace of God everything was called off and we arrived back at barracks at 4am in a sodden condition. The whole business was quite awful.'

The only military occasions when he did enjoy himself was when he was flying with the RAF, working with the Palestine Police or spending time with friends in either the Transjordan Frontier Force or the Sudanese Camel Corps. Both of these formations were led by British Army officers on secondment. They enjoyed more freedom than in a regular formation and had the added benefit of still being mounted on horses. On a number of occasions during his time in the Middle East my father thought seriously of a three year secondment to either of them as a way to get away from regimental soldiering, gain additional allowances and enable him to ride every day:

'I'm seriously considering applying to go into the Transjordan Frontier Force it seems a grand life – one becomes a cavalry officer for 4 years.'

He described his attachment to the RAF (No.14 Squadron):

'Here I am a real outposter of the Empire. It really is great fun, very interesting, most amusing and flying gives me rather a thrill. Well, I'll begin at the beginning. We started off from Kalundia a landing ground just outside Jerusalem. We flew over amazing country – brown hills and rocks which looked just like those brown raised maps we had at school – over the Jordan Valley quite close to the Dead Sea and then again over more hills even browner than the first and finally landed up here – Amman is the capital of TJ (Trans Jordan) and the Emir Abdulla and all his court live here – in the middle of the town is a Roman amphitheatre quite a good one I believe – the RAF station is stuck on a hill right on the outskirts on the edge of the desert more brown hills rather lower without a scrap of vegetation of any sort they just go on and on for miles and miles

– the whole place is full of remains of various sorts and as one goes over it changes colour due to the different sorts of rocks so you can tell fairly well where you are just by that.

Well the same morning I was whisked away into the air again and set off to visit the Police posts in the northern half of the Jordan valley – on the way we passed Aylun castle an old Crusader place really wonderful and quite well preserved – Jerash which is full of Roman remains and which you certainly must see if you come, a forum, amphitheatre and masses of buildings columns etc really amazing. It was rather bumpy and circling round Police posts rather lowdown proved too much for Fass who was violently sick at each Police post we came to but I've got over that now. Everywhere one goes one sees remains of some sort or another. TJ was *the* corn growing part in Roman times. Next day we visited landing grounds also in the Jordan valley and went to Beisan where on top of a hill there is the remains of a whole old city. Then we went and watched bombs being dropped in the desert – they go off with an alarming vivacity I'd hate to be underneath one at any time. Yesterday we went out to a place called Asrack and pretended we'd broken down and another plane came out and rescued us and after that we went for a tour round the desert. Well I'm off to change for dinner. I'll let you know when I use my parachute!'

There was however much sporting activity to make up for the poor quality of soldiering and my father took full advantage of it. There was hunting jackals with the Hunt to which he quickly became whipper-in and general dogsbody to the Master who was head of the Palestine Police. He wrote:

'We'd a great hunt last Sunday and Fass more by luck that good judgement is the blue eyed whip to the Master.'

The officers of the Battalion formed a polo team which competed against other units in the area and he also played for the local club. Much of his time was spent looking after his own mounts, schooling other officers' polo ponies or scheming how to buy or sell nags that others had abandoned as being no good. These included Freckle, Cuthbert and

Percy all of whom served their purpose as ponies and hunters. He and what he called "his brave warriors" would take a broken hunter, jumper or polo pony in hand, train or re-train it and then either ride it himself or re-sell it. This was also one way that he managed his budget. Sometimes he involved his mother who would finance the initial purchase of the pony or horse by sending him a money order and then be paid back when it was sold at a profit:

'I've bought a pony, he's really rather nice but very young, only 3 ½ which is silly but he's the sort of horse that takes one's eye straight away and I just had to buy him regardless of his tender years. He's a grey rather than a rusty grey with a very fine head and a flowing mane and tail. I got him fairly cheap and bargained the man down from £45 to £25 which wasn't too bad. I honestly think he ought to turn out rather well and with a bit of luck should make a bit of money on him........If I can possibly afford it which I doubt I want to buy a very tumbledown (polo) pony for £10, at the present moment it's an absolute skeleton it's not been fed for about two months and looks quite awful but I think it might have possibilities and it would be rather fun to see if one could do anything with it.'

There were also numerous target shooting and show jumping competitions and gymkhanas in which he competed either on his own horse or those of others, including the General's. He shot a great variety of birds whenever he could that included sand grouse and every other creature that flew in the air unless he was shooting with the French in which case birds were taken by them whilst on the ground! He described one such shooting expedition:

'I went up to Lake Heule which is north of the Sea of Galilee to shoot duck and that was rather fun. It's 140 miles from Jerusalem and when the duck are in is just stiff with them I believe but we actually were rather too early and didn't see many. We got 7 I think and 2 snipe.'

On another occasion he wrote:

'We shot each afternoon – the first day Monday went up to a bog north of Jaffa and got 2 duck and 4 ½ brace of snipe – Tuesday another bog got 7 brace of quail 2 brace of duck and a couple of snipe – the next day on the same place 7 ½ couple of snipe, 1 duck and 2 brace of quail so that was grand – Thursday I went out cub-hunting and today went out after partridges without success. Next week to a place called Azrack in the desert on a large shoot – the AOC and lord knows who.'

He swam at seaside camp with 85 of his men at Athulit and sailed on Lake Galilee. He described a typical jumping competition:

'There were some Police sports here on Thursday and they were rather fun. I was jumping a charger in the Open and having done fairly well in the morning and got into the final, eight were left in, nothing went right at all in the afternoon and I got 8 faults a round which did not win me the cup however it was great fun and something to have got into the final.'

At a rifle meeting at Sarafand he met with "unqualified" success for his team's point of view (HQ Wing):

'We won the Wauchope (the Governer's) cup as a Company and the Revolver and made quite a lot of money in prizes – I happened to strike a good patch and won the highest individual score at 600x with a record score of 7 bulls and 3 inners – next day managed to keep it up and shooting for Palestine in an open cup against the West Indies and other colonies got top score and got another record at 500x this time 8 bulls and 2 inners – was top also in the Revolver team and so had quite a successful 3 days.'

His social life was very restricted to a small group of local military and civilian families stationed in the country most of whom he found "deadbeat". He often asked his mother if these were the same kind of people that she had had to put up with when she lived in Khartoum! There were few *lovelies* available and he found the Americans much more fun to be with than his own countrymen and women. He wrote to his mother:

'I think I told you about the bathing party under the Mediterranean moon with the Americans and helped with vodka and caviar it was about the best party there's been out here. The Americans are about the only people who've got any life in them at all and continually say the most priceless things.'

Perhaps it was this positive experience of being with these Americans that would later help him to make the relationships with their countrymen that would be so critical for his work as a D-Day planner in 1943-44.

A letter to his mother describes his first Christmas overseas:

'I'm sorry to say I had a very alcoholic Christmas – it simply was unavoidable the troops of course love it and part of the performance is to see how much their officers can imbibe without showing it unduly. Christmas Eve I went to Midnight Mass at Bethlehem and thereby got enough religion to last me for the rest of the year. I went at 10.30 and couldn't get out until 2 in the morning!! At first it was all rather interesting – typically Eastern – a church with very beautiful things in it – very old – with thousands of Greek Orthodox and Armenian churchmen all in wonderful clothes - incense – thousands of candles and whatnot all most impressive – but if one looked up at the roof one found it full of holes – the walls were all stained where water had come in and the church was full of a heterogeneous collection of Arabs, Egyptians, French, our own troops – Jewish women talking at the tops their voices, eating things out of paper bags and chewing – occasionally there would be a frightful uproar from one part of the church or another where someone had pushed too hard – whereupon everyone would look round and gape like people in charabancs – the service was amazing – one priest all in red and his underlings who continually took off and replaced their hats and who undressed and dressed in fresh clothes every five minutes. I was alright for an hour but frightful for 3 ½ and the seats were dismally hard and one wriggled all the time.

On Christmas Day we visited the Sergeants Mess and then our own Companies. Had the most enormous lunch in our Mess and finished off the day by going to the King David (Hotel) for a wild and woolly dance which went on until 4 o'clock in the morning. Boxing Day we had some donkey races in the afternoon which were great fun and had the Married people of the Regiment in to dinner in the evening.'

It was in the dog days after Christmas that he became rather gloomy as he wrote to his mother:

'Rather a dull week with no news of any description – I've done nothing at all and until last night when I went out to the King David (Hotel) and danced in a terribly boring and uninteresting party had not left barracks ever since the previous Friday. I've got another fit of the dumps actually there is simply nothing to do - one might shoot but to do that one must have a car. My pony also is lame with a big knee. It got loose due to a thoroughly inefficient groom and proceeded to jump the water trough slipped on the concrete the other side and took the most frightful fall. It was lucky the big knee was the only damage. I haven't been able to hunt as since last Sunday I haven't been able to get a pony to ride in fact life is very dismal.'

The winter weather in Palestine did not help to raise his morale:

'For the last three weeks it has been bitterly cold and from last Friday to the following Tuesday it rained incessantly – not just ordinary rain but the stuff that gets you drenched in 30 seconds. It came in through the shut windows of my room – through the roof, everywhere. The Mess was filled with buckets catching streams of water that came into almost every room. The railway from Haifa was washed away and still is so. 3 bridges on the road thither are now non-existent and a mountain moved wholesale onto the road. All the telephone wires went and here in the Mess all the lights went out.'

He also spent time sightseeing throughout Palestine. His mother was an amateur archaeologist and he often referred to trips to the Holy Places and Biblical sights as well as to the great Crusader castles. On several occasions he camped inside their walls and wrote about these experiences:

'Last Sunday we went down to the Dead Sea and saw old Jericho which was rather interesting, merely a mound of earth etc with various bits of walls and corner stones which had been uncovered. On the way back we had a look at the Castle of Blood, am old Crusader castle now all tumbled down but one could still see the vaulted roofs and wall.'

On another occasion he visited the coast:

'A place called Aquib where we had some manoeuvres one day was most interesting, the last Crusader castle to hold out in Palestine. It was right at the end of an isthmus and until 1810 was in first class repair but some old Turk wanted to repair Acre and instead of quarrying new stone merely smashed down part of the castle. Then on the other side there were some more remains of a heap with channels cut to catch the rainwater and cisterns. An antiquary who was there said that Richard C de L had had breakfast there after fighting somewhere. We also went to a castle which is now a prison at Acre with an old 13th century fountain which is still in use and a magnificent garden. Just outside we went to see the Crypt of St John which was an amazing place, a crusader church which is now below the level of the street.'

On a sightseeing tour of Lake Tiberias he reported:

'At one place there was an old stone cistern or bath washed down (the hillside) and I went up to have a look at it and found the remains of what must have been a Roman villa or something rather amazing – 2 of these sort of stone sinks and cornices and a broken pillar. I searched about for coins and things but couldn't find any – you'd have loved it – I found one or two bits of glass and pottery but nothing worth keeping at all.

His parents, now Sir Ernest and Lady Fass, visited him in Jerusalem in September 1935 and at Christmas he was in Alexandria with his sister Maria and her husband Brian who were stationed there at the time. His youngest sister Susan also visited again.

Romance

At the same time as leading a busy and active life as a member of the Battalion, my father had begun to think seriously about Elizabeth Verey whom he had met in the Spring of 1934. Whilst it is quite likely that they had met again before he left England in September of that year, the romance had not really *taken off* at this stage. We shall never know precisely what it was that had attracted them to each other initially and we have only their early correspondence to guide us.

Their relationship got off to a somewhat rocky start as it was conducted at a distance when my father was serving overseas and my mother lived in London and at Bridge House, Twyford, the town and country homes of her parents in Berkshire. There were therefore frequent opportunities for misunderstanding. He continued to dabble in light affairs with a number of locally-based *lovelies,* whilst my mother, aged 26, had been in danger of being compromised by falling in love with a young Royal Navy officer stationed in the Mediterranean. This individual had not been able to return her affections and her father had been obliged to intervene on her behalf and to ascertain if the young man had serious intentions, which he did not.

Worse was to follow. My father got wind of an unfortunate remark made about Elizabeth by an officer in another regiment of the same intake as his at the RMC who had recently arrived in the Middle East. It was to the effect that she was a tease who had *come on* at him during a dance in London. My father wrote to ask her if there was any truth in the charge, because if so their brief liaison would be ended. When she denied it, my father responded that she had clearly been insulted and threatened to kill the offender! The officer in question would later become a famously unpopular wartime general of paratroops.

My father was attractive, glamorous and had a sense of humour. He was funny, a good mimic, wore his heart on his sleeve and was more extravert than Elizabeth. He engaged readily with others and loved all outdoors activities and sports, especially riding. In contrast my mother was enigmatic, slender, serious, intellectual and more intraverted than him. She internalised her feelings and expressed them in her love of art, literature, languages and music. She found it more difficult to express her emotions openly. Her favourite opera was the great romantic tragedy *Die Meistersingers.* My sister Ginny once asked my mother about the way that she and my father had expressed themselves in their letters. My mother replied that he declared his love for her passionately and often but that she had did not find it easy to respond in the same way in their correspondence although she clearly adored him and often spoke of her deep love for him.

A typical example of this difference in their characters was his reaction to Charles Morgan's romantic novel *Sparkenbroke* which she had sent out for him to read in Palestine. It was my mother's favourite book and she loved it; was this was some kind of test he had to pass? His response was that he thought it was soppy and its hero effete. If this was the kind of thing she liked, he doubted if there was a future for their relationship! He tested her in his turn by writing to her about his love for Scotland and of all its sporting opportunities; fishing, shooting, stalking, etc. She said she hated the place. Nothing but rain and mosquitoes!

Alexandria

He was due 80 days leave in October 1935 and had been greatly looking forward to going home to England for a time but the situation in the Middle East deteriorated and his leave was cancelled much to his dismay. After 15 months in Jerusalem, in December 1935, the Battalion was transferred to Egypt and sent to the port of Alexandria to be stationed at Mustapha Barracks. My father described the move to his mother:

'I was baggage officer and so rather hard worked before-hand getting everything in and then was sort of Adjutant on the 2nd train and had to make arrangements and all, We arrived at 2.30 in the morning after a bitter journey crossed the Canal and got here at 10 o'clock. Then until 7 at night I was coping with awful baggage. After Jerusalem this place is the absolute metropolis our eyes pop out of our heads at the trams and all the well dressed women and the Club and the Cabarets and all but it looks like being very expensive and except for an awful sand track round the Sporting Club, no-where to ride.'

Fortunately, his sister Maria and brother in law Brian had been posted to the Fleet in Alexandria so they were able to see each other frequently. My father reported that:

'I've never seen any people quite so absurdly in love as she and Brain and it is simply grand having Maria here and we shall have a terrific party (at Christmas) but there is not a *lovely* in the place and in any event the mere army would not have a look in against the host of nautics that besiege the town'.

His cousin Rodney *Odds* Wrightson was also in port serving on HMS London and my father went on board for cocktails in the Wardroom on several occasions.

The Italians had invaded Abyssinia in October 1935 and the British Government was intent on reinforcing its troops in the Middle East in anticipation of more trouble from Mussolini and in Palestine:

'The war scare here is incredible and people expect quite firmly that we shall be involved in January. I personally think that it is my eye but at least this time the army don't look as of they are going to be caught out. At all events I hate this conglomerated mass of militarism and wish myself well back in England as soon as possible.'

He still hoped for home leave in late 1935 and early 1936 but with shipping crowding the harbour and the Battalion acting as guards for the vast quantities of goods being landed, this would be unlikely.

Training also continued as the idea of the potential for future conflicts began to penetrate the Army's mind and it began to anticipate the end of the long decline in its capabilities that had lasted for the past ten years. However, the posting at Alexandria was temporary and in March 1936 after three months in the port city, the Battalion was transferred to its more permanent home still in Egypt but in the Canal Zone at Moascar.

Moascar & the Canal Zone
To be stationed at Moascar would have been a very different experience for my father. The Battalion was part of the Canal Brigade commanded by Brigadier F Pile of the Royal Tank Corps and was one of the few in

the British Army to be mechanised. This meant that its deployment was mobile and its training was much more realistic of future warfare than that in which my father had previously participated. At the outbreak of war the brigade was renamed and numbered First Armoured Brigade and was to fight throughout the Desert Campaign in the Middle East. Pile and his Brigade Major, Sandy Galloway were enthusiasts of armoured warfare; the concentration of force that it allowed and of rapid movement on the battlefield. Both were to rise to high rank in the coming war and my father may well have been influenced by their thinking and leadership. In their turn, they may have spotted his potential as he was to serve with Galloway later in his career. However, the Canal Brigade was an exception. Since the First World War, because of the parlous state of the Army, training was carried out mainly at Battalion level and few senior officers had any experience of higher command or the management of larger formations. This was to have dire consequences for the early direction of the war as commanders simply did not have the skills to lead these larger units.

Kitchener Lines in which the Battalion was stationed was a bare barracks of wooden huts with asbestos roofs but with two cinemas and a good sports ground. At various times the Battalion had to find detachments for a small garrison on Cyprus (to which his friend *Mac* Macdowel was posted) and troops for Port Said which made training in larger numbers both difficult and unrealistic. New equipment had begun to arrive as the Army re-armed and this involved the training of transport drivers and mortar men although the Battalion still relied on a total of 176 animals for its baggage train.

In addition to individual training, there were more sports, athletics and sailing on the nearby salt lakes as well as competition with neighbouring troops including those of the French forces with whom Great Britain shared the responsibility for the security of the Suez Canal.

Whilst the main task of the Brigade was the defence of the Suez Canal and its environs, it could also be used if trouble broke out anywhere else in the Near East and in May 1936 the Battalion was ordered to return to Palestine at the start of the Arab Revolt. Detachments were sent up to Haifa and elsewhere to guard strong points and prepare camps for the arrival of the First Division who were en route from England. Thereafter these returned to Moascar. My father reported:

'I've seen one of two people who have just come down from Palestine and they say the whole thing is being grossly mismanaged and is completely futile and all these troops are needed to quell at most 300-400 Arabs. It's quite absurd.'

However, in October 1936, whilst the Battalion completed its Near East tour before proceeding to India in October 1937, my father was posted home as Adjutant to the Regimental Depot at Brock Barracks in Reading and as a result he did not follow the Battalion to its last pre-war station at Lucknow in India. He was not to serve with the Second Battalion, the Royal Berkshire Regiment (Princess Charlotte of Wales's) again and his military career was to take a different path in the future.

The Battalion had been my father's home for the past five years and he had benefited from and contributed to the continuity of both its traditions and its standards. It had also been a time during which he had developed his military skills in leadership, training and in the management of men under arms. The British Army's Regiments of the Line passed into history many years ago when they were considered to be no longer needed to guard Great Britain's empire or fight its wars. Through a brutal and continual process of amalgamations and disbandments, the Royal Berkshire Regiment has long since ceased to exist and has a place only in the hearts and minds of those who served in the Regiment and of their descendants. Two writers have commented on the demise of these regiments, one describing his wartime service with the Second Battalion of the Regiment in Burma and the other following service in Korea with the Royal Ulster Rifles in the immediate post-war period:

'.... In a battalion of British infantry such as ourselves, it was the regimental tradition, for those of us who professed to be Royal Berkshiremen, that kept us going when times were hard. Across the County of Berkshire, in Newbury, Pangbourne, Twyford, Maidenhead, Wokingham, Aldermaston, on the Berkshire Downs and in all the villages along the route of the old A4 trunk road, there was no one in the county or who visited the county town of

Reading who had not seen or heard of the massive memorial lion erected to all those men of the 66th (Berkshire) Regiment who fell at the battle of Maiwand. The knowledge that throughout the ages.... the regiment had, in the eyes of the world, fought according to the highest traditions of the service, both in defeat and in victory, was our foundation and inspiration.' (Hill)

and

'Serving soldiers are taciturn men, certainly not given to public utterance. When they do speak out, it usually lands them in trouble. Servants to politicians, they pick up the pieces when others have made a mess....Abroad, they accepted conditions in dust-dried barracks that would have brought shop stewards to apoplexy. During the Sixties they became the butt of satirist and cineastes: rich young men who have done well out of the peace...If they were short on original ideas and lacked imagination, they had other qualities easy to overlook in the age of affluence. Unselfishness, for instance; a personal code of honour; a stubborn integrity; a rooted tendency to keep their word. Unfashionable qualities, now in short supply, not over-abundant among smooth men in the media.' (Ions)

These military institutions and their histories represented something precious and important in our national culture and I am proud that my father had the honour of serving in the 'Old 66th'.

Chapter Six
ADJUTANTCY,
MARRIAGE & INSTRUCTOR

Adjutancy

It is a mark of the regard in which a young officer is held by his Regiment that he is appointed as one of its adjutants as this was considered to be the first step for a young officer with ambition who aspired to achieve higher command. It was given to the most promising officers in their rank at the time and after careful consideration by their seniors.

My father served as an Adjutant on a number of occasions that included the role of acting Adjutant to the Second Battalion of the Regiment in Alexandria and Moascar and as Adjutant of its Regimental Depot in Reading for two years between October 1936 and December 1938.

An Adjutant was the colonel's personal staff officer and principal assistant who implemented his orders and managed all the details of the daily organisation and discipline of the junior officers, NCOs and enlisted men. In war and on manoeuvres he prepared the operation orders that would convert the colonel's battle plans into exact detail. In barracks, the Adjutant's principal concerns were dress, drill, discipline, military law, all forms of ceremonial and the management of the band and corps of drums. As a way to appreciate my father's role as Adjutant, Masters in *Bugles and a Tiger* described the personal transformation that occurred when he exchanged his position as the senior subaltern in one of its two battalions for that of the Adjutant of the Regimental Depot, 4th Prince of Wales Ghurka Rifles in the Indian Army, in which he served:

'To fulfil his responsibilities an adjutant had to know everything, forget nothing and forgive nothing. It was a most prized appointment and was usually held for four years in peacetime. There were many ways of being a good adjutant, but several factors were common to all of them, and the first three were that one must lose all sense of humour, all sense of proportion and all desire to win or keep friends. The adjutant was the man whose eyes lit up when he discovered some tiny peccadillo, who poured on it the scorn and the horror the colonel must reserve for greater catastrophes. He was the man whose watch was right to within one second and drove himself into a paroxysm of rage if someone else thought that ten seconds more or less did not matter. The adjutant knew all the correct abbreviations and forms and procedures and did not allow himself to think whether any of them were perhaps slightly ridiculous.' (Masters)

My father's duty as Adjutant of the Regimental Depot was to be responsible for a variety of activities that lay at the centre of the Regiment's traditions and efforts. The main task of the Depot was to take new recruits into its ranks and to train them for whatever service the Regiment might be called on to perform.

The Depot also provided training for newly appointed NCOs and for the members of the Regiment's volunteer battalions. At the Depot standards of drill were, if that were possible, even higher than in its two battalions and its staff prided themselves on turning raw recruits into useful soldiers whose contribution would be especially remarked upon when they arrived at their first posting with one of the two service battalions. The Depot also housed the Regimental museum in which its most precious trophies were held and on its parade ground stood the Memorial to its fallen of the 1914-18 war. Masters again:

'Now it was I who glided around the parade ground, communing in silent scorn with a regimental deity who inhabited the middle air a hundred feet above my head. The young soldiers blinked in awe at my glassy boots and leggings, the beautiful sword at my waist, its leather wrist strap flopping long and loose to show that I was the adjutant. They were amazed to see that before my feet paths became smooth, doors opened, walls vanished. Potholes were filled up. I never looked down, around, or about and I never tripped or stumbled' (Masters).

In addition, when its battalions were either serving overseas or garrisoned away from the County, the Depot was responsible for all matters concerning the Regiment's ceremonial duties; represented the Regiment locally and was expected to ensure that a high profile was maintained both as an aid to recruiting and to put the Regiment's best foot forward to the public throughout the regimental area, an activity known as *Showing the flag.*

These appearances included attendance at Reading and Bicester agricultural shows and the Newbury racing festival as well as numerous local town and village fetes across the County that involved physical training displays, boxing matches and the music of the Regimental Band and Drums. As Adjutant my father would have been involved with and responsible for the organisation of all such events and in October 1936 was responsible for the Regiment's detachment on the occasion of the Coronation of George VI. Other typical social events included the Regimental garden party, the dining-in of a new Lord Lieutenant and the Judges of the Assizes as well as a Copenhagen Ball in the Sergeants' Mess that commemorated the 49th Regiment's service as marines in Nelson's victorious sea battle of 1801.

In addition, each year the Depot organised an *At Home* to which the public were invited to watch the army at work and play. In the summer of 1935, the year before my father arrived, there were 3120 visitors; in 1936, 8000 and in 1937, 17,600. These increases were one sign of the British people waking up to the threat of another war. Likewise, recruiting began to pick up with 125 recruits in 1935; 149 in 1936, rising to 190 in 1938.

In response to the worsening situation in Europe attempts were made to strengthen the Army and a number of categories of reserves were introduced. Some were time-served soldiers who had previously retired but undertook extra years of duty and others who had no previous military experience joined up for one year of which the first six months were spent at the Depot. All of this led to increased activity at the Depot between 1936-1938 which was during the time of my father's service.

Marriage

One reason that my father found his posting to the Depot back in England a congenial prospect was that it would enable him to pursue the romance that he had started with Elizabeth Verey whilst he had been serving overseas. My mother used to tell the story of being invited to lunch on his return for the first time with him and his parents, Sir Ernest and Lady Fass. She set off in her father's car from Twyford to drive the 30 miles westwards along the A4 to Inkpen. She reached Hungerford and shortly afterwards took a left- hand turn signposted for Kintbury and Inkpen. Soon after, a figure appeared walking briskly towards her. As the individual got closer she recognised my father who, unable to contain his anticipation at seeing her again, had walked the four miles from the house to surprise her on the road. I think that there may have been some dilly-dallying at the hedgerow-side on the way back to Foxhill and that it was at this moment that Elizabeth knew that she was in love with her *Johnny.*

The path of true love was not however to be smooth and a number of serious obstacles to marriage would need to be overcome. The first of these objections were military. British Army and regimental regulations laid down that a young officer could not be married until he attained the rank of Captain, had completed at least nine years of service and had received the permission of his commanding officer. My father did not qualify on any of these counts: he would not be promoted Captain until January 1939; he had only five years service and the permission of his commanding officer, Major Hight, in command at the Depot, would not immediately be forthcoming,

The second were the objections of his father. Ernest maintained that my father had given his word to the Regiment that he would remain single whilst Adjutant of the Depot and that he would be breaking it by getting married. In addition, Ernest advised my father that he did not have the means to afford married life and that he, Ernest, would not support him further financially. Elizabeth's father, Henry Verey, could do so if he wished. This caused a serious rift between my father and mother and Sir Ernest which, I believe, was never repaired.

Although my father had only returned from Egypt to take up his post in October 1936, by December of that year he was already trying to work out how he and Elizabeth could be married. First, there was the Army.

There is a handwritten note of my father's which provides the detailed view of his commanding officer. Whether Major Hight had invited my father to present his arguments from a superior's perspective or whether the note was written as an aide memoire by my father before or after meeting the Major to discuss the matter, we shall never know. I suspect the latter! The note read as follows:

```
9.12.36
Appreciation of the situation

1.   My private opinion
Like you to be happy and contented
2.   My official view must be
(a)  What does Col. Leslie think!
Does he entirely approve!
(b)  Have you the whole-hearted approval and support of
your father

Provided I am satisfied with the answers of 2 (a) and
(b) then my decision must necessarily be after careful
consideration :-
3.   If you remain at the Depot
(a)  A promise not to get married until after 31ˢᵗ
December 1937
(b)  A promise not to get married until I am satisfied
that your financial situation permits it to be possible
(c)  If you guarantee 3 (a) and (b) above then I approve
of your "Engagement" being officially announced in the
papers

4.   My reasons for my views:-
(a)  Before accepting the Depot Adjutancy you should have
intimated your intentions
(b)  The accepted rule that I have been used to is that
```

no officer under 29 should ask his CO for permission to
marry unless he can produce some exceptional reason
(c) The Depot Mess is a very small community and the
very minimum of dining members is 3. If you get married
it would reduce our Depot Mess to 2 dining members

5.   If you do not accept my decision I must in all
fairness to myself and all the Depot officers request
for your immediate return to the 2nd Bn. And a relief
dispatched forthwith to take your place

6.   I applied for you to be Adjutant because I thought
(a) You had no intention of marriage
(b) You would hunt with the South Berks
(c) You would take the Staff College Exam in February
1938

Signed PH Hight

There were two issues of particular concern. The first was the issue of
the approval of his father, which he knew he did not yet have and the
second was the implied threat of being returned to the Battalion which
would be a seriously adverse mark on his Army record.

The key thing now was to persuade his father that marriage to Elizabeth
was what he wanted and that his father should both approve of it and
provide the financial support that would be needed. He would then
have to convince Major Hight that his work at the Depot would not be
affected.

Whilst my father's romance with Elizabeth may not have been of the
whirlwind variety, he certainly lost no time in pursuing his aim. He
had returned to England in October 1936, met up with Elizabeth again
shortly afterwards, confirmed to his satisfaction that he wanted to marry
her and lost no time in laying his plans. Although the memorandum to
or for Major Hight referred to an engagement that would be permitted
in one year's time in December 1937, with any marriage scheduled for
1938, the idea of waiting that long clearly held no appeal for him. In
November 1936, before the Hight memo had even been written, my
father opened up his campaign, not quite two months after returning
from the Middle East and taking up his appointment as Adjutant.

There are nine letters remaining from his father Sir Ernest which detail his objections to the marriage and each one is increasingly acrimonious with regards to my father's plans and their financial and career implications. Amongst the exchanges that took place were included discussion of my father's overall financial position, the fact that he could not afford the costs of married life and that Sir Ernest was not prepared to subsidise it beyond the allowance that he contributed already which was £100 per year.

Next came a proposal from my father that he would leave the service and get a civilian job. Sir Ernest riposted that jobs in England were scarce; that my mother and father would have to make a career in the Colonies where the cost of living would be lower or that my father would have to start at the bottom as a travelling salesman for Shell! The Verey family tried to help with an introduction by Cyprian Bridge, a close family friend, to Messels the stockbrokers, who might be looking for a 'novice' and by Michael Verey at Helbert Wagg & Co, investment bankers, who suggested that my father should meet a contact at Lucas Industries. As it turned out, the idea of a career outside of the Army would not be discussed again until 1944 when my mother speculated that when the war had ended my father should consider becoming 'something big in plastics'.

The matter of an engagement ring caused the most disagreement. The cost was £45 which my father did not have and asked Sir Ernest to help pay for it. Sir Ernest responded that if my father could not even afford his own ring that it was preposterous that he should think of getting married! He would subscribe not more than £30 towards it but that this amount would be taken off the annual allowance, thereby making it even more difficult for my father to make ends meet at the start of his married life. Finally, as far as Sir Ernest was concerned, my father had broken his word to the Regiment and to Hight that he would remain single and live in the Mess for the three years of his service there and that Ernest did not think much of the breach of trust that this would represent.

However the correspondence ended in April 1937 with Ernest's reluctant acquiescence and Hight's agreement to the marriage so that all obstacles appear to have been overcome and my father's engagement to Elizabeth was announced in The Times in the spring of 1937.

They were married on the 3rd June at St Paul's Church, Knightsbridge and spent their honeymoon at Portofino in Italy. His best friend from the Regiment *Mac* Macdowel should have acted as his best man but he was unavailable so another brother officer stood in for him. On their arrival in Italy they telegraphed Inkpen with the news: "Excellent journey marvellous place love Fasses." The report on their marriage in the Reading Mercury carried the headline "Berks Adjutant wed in London – County families distinguished guests." On their return they rented a house, 'Mapletons', close by the Depot on Lord Iliffe's estate at Yattendon. From all that my mother said, they settled down blissfully to married life together.

My mother used to tell two stories about their early time together. The first was about my father's inability to manage his budget which was to become a recurring theme throughout their marriage and often referred to later in their wartime correspondence. After they had been married for one or two months, my father failed to provide the monthly housekeeping allowance and when asked by my mother where it had got to responded that there could not be any that month because he had needed to "order a suit to be made by his tailor for going out to lunch in the country on Sundays!"

The second story was about the first occasion on which the newly married couple asked my father's Fass parents to come to Sunday lunch from Inkpen. My mother got up very early to prepare lunch before driving over to her parents home at Twyford to borrow a parlour maid who would help at table. In the middle of lunch her new mother in law turned around to her son, my father, and asked: "And are you getting enough to eat, Dear?" After they had left, this caused a tremendous row but had a happy ending. The following year on the occasion of my mother's birthday on the 15th April 1938, my father gave my mother a voucher for six cookery lesson at the Cordon Blue School in London and my mother's cooking never looked back!

On the occasion of his marriage my father received the following from his tailor in Egypt:

'Dear Master,
As I came to know from your batman (Pte. Setchell) that master has been married.
I am much happy at this news and request you and Mrs. Fass to receive my best regards and congratulations for this happy marriage.
May God bestow you and Mrs. a long life and prosperity. Thanking you always for your favours and kindness.
Yours faithfully,
Mohammed Amin (Indian master tailor)
2nd Royal Berkshire Regt.
Moascar Ismailia
Kitchener Lines'

Whatever the difficulties that had arisen over my father's marriage they did not seem to affect the high esteem in which Major Hight held him. After ten months in post, my father received his first annual report covering the period 23rd October 1936, the date of his appointment to the Depot, to 31st August 1937. The report read:

This officer has been my Adjutant for the past ten
months. I have found him to be extremely intelligent,
hardworking and tactful. He has performed his duties in a
most conscientious and efficient manner and has displayed
excellent organising ability.
He has a great deal of character and is gifted with a
charming personality which he uses to the best advantage
when dealing with both Officers and Other Ranks.
A good sportsman and a very fine horseman. An excellent
Regimental Officer in every respect whom I strongly
recommend as being a suitable candidate for admission to
the Staff College.

The 1937 report was the first occasion on which my father showed his ambition to gain a place on the Army's coveted Staff College course which at that time lasted for two years. If successful he could expect to join the 1938 intake. Admission to and graduation from the Staff College was the next milestone of achievement after the Adjutancy for an officer with ambition and talent. Thereafter it provided access to positions on the general staff. Passed Staff College or *psc* after an officer's name in the Army List was the mark of an individual who stood a chance of promotion to the highest ranks of the Army and was a most sought after qualification. This first application was not successful.

In the following year on the 25th May 1938 my mother gave birth to their first child, my eldest sister Serena, who they both thought was perfection. In September 1938 they took a holiday in Europe – their last abroad as it was to turn out – and travelled across France to Switzerland where they visited the Martin-Achard, Dominice, Junod and Lenoir families in Geneva with whom my mother had lived as a young woman. In the middle of the holiday my father received a telegram which read *Return to barracks, Hight.* It was the beginning of the Munich crisis and the outbreak of war was expected. They had to cut short their holiday and hurry home. Whilst the immediate threat of war was settled by appeasing Hitler, the crisis was a sign of the storm that was to break over Europe less than a year later.

Meanwhile, my father continued to serve at the Depot through 1938 and in August of that year he received his second confidential report from Major Hight:

```
'An extremely efficient, intelligent and capable officer.
He has been my Adjutant for the past 2 years during
which period he has proved himself to be an officer of
outstanding qualities. He accepts responsibility. Has
initiative and is gifted with a very quick brain.  He
is very smart in appearance, has an athletic figure and
is full of zeal and energy. A very good horseman and an
excellent sportsman. The best type of Regimental officer
who should rise to the highest ranks in the Army. I
strongly recommend him as candidate eminently suitable
for admission to the Staff College.

PH Hight, Major
```

and

```
'I agree. A very able officer who should make an
excellent staff officer
```

(Major General Butler was an officer of the Royal Warwickshire Regiment who had commanded forces in Iraq and the Middle East. At the time, he was commanding the 48th South Midlands Division a TA formation with whom my father completed a staff attachment in March 1938)

This was the second reference for admission to the Staff College now planned for the 1939 intake. However, after fifteen months as Adjutant at the Depot, in December 1938 my father was promoted to Captain and posted as an Instructor to the Royal Military College that he had left seven years earlier. For an officer of his rank this was a very prestigious appointment.

Instructor

The position of Instructor was given to the most outstanding of the British Army's younger officers and the regimental historian recorded the fact that in that year (1938) the Regiment had achieved a record number of five students to the Staff College and two instructors from the Depot to the RMC, of which my father was one. It would be fair to say that in this new appointment his military career was on its way and that his skill and experience in the training of soldiers was by now acknowledged by his superiors as being of the highest quality demanded.

The Commandant of the College was Major General T R Eastwood of the Rifle Brigade and the Adjutant was Captain E H Goulburn of the Grenadier Guards who later commanded their First Battalion in Normandy. My father was posted to No. 1 Company commanded by Major R Peake of the Royal Scots. There were a total of sixty three officers on the College staff of whom twenty seven were Instructors drawn from the regiments of the British and Indian armies and responsible for c. 1050 cadets in three divisions. A fellow Instructor in No. 1 Company, of whom my mother used to speak as a particular friend of my father's, was Bernard Fergusson of the Black Watch who was later to attend the Staff College with my father in 1941 and to achieve fame as the leader of one of the Chindit columns in Burma.

The life of an Instructor at the RMC was relentless but fun. By the beginning of 1939 it was clear to most of the population that there would be a second war and both the Instructors and the cadets must have been very aware of this as they dashed about the place from parade ground to class room and from PT to the riding school. My father's appointment had referred to a requirement to instruct in current affairs so he would have needed to keep himself up to date with daily events in Europe. The issues that my father would have needed to deal with in his lectures would have included Germany's warlike intentions following Hitler's re-entry into the Sudetenland that divided Czechoslovakia; the Austrian *Anschlus;* the annexation of Danzig and the threatened invasion of Poland, all of which acts presaged the outbreak of war that came in September.

By the outbreak of war my father and mother had enjoyed two years of marriage in peacetime. The remainder of their time together was to be spent entirely in wartime Britain and they were never again to experience anything like a normal married life. My father had also expanded his network of colleagues in the Army, a number of whom were to be of importance to him for his future.

Chapter Seven
WAR & THE WELSH GUARDS

War

War was declared on the 3rd September 1939 and, as in the First World War, the RMC was broken up into a number of Officer Cadet Training Units (OCTU) as a way to deal with the great increase required in the production of officers for wartime service. In October, because of his current appointment at the RMC, my father was posted as a Company Commander to one of the first three of these units, 162 OCTU located at Bulford Camp on Salisbury Plain. Its first cadets were drawn from the Honourable Artillery Company (HAC), the world's oldest regiment based in the City of London that had a long tradition of acting as an officer cadet training establishment for young men working in the City.

The Company had c. 130 cadets and their programme was reduced from two years to six months. The pace was intensive and my father reported to my mother that he was being run ragged. One particular difficulty was dealing with those who would not be recommended for a Commission. Some of his colleagues found the decision to return a cadet to his unit (RTU) a simple matter but my father agonised over it knowing full well the effect that it would have on the individuals concerned.

The Welsh Guards

Shortly after my father was posted to the OCTU a major change took place in his military fortunes. Since at least 1938 the writing had been on the wall as regards the coming conflict with Germany and the British Army had been instructed to make plans for its expansion in the event of war. At the outbreak of war each regiment would be ordered to create additional battalions consisting of both volunteers and conscripted men stiffened with a backbone of regulars. These new recruits could be expected to have little or no previous military experience and a cadre of experienced officers and NCOs to train and lead them would be required.

My father's long held ambition had been to join the Brigade of Guards. The Brigade was both socially and soldierly the elite of the British Army.

As has been already recorded, his mother's family regiment was the Coldstream Guards that he had not been able to join in 1931 when he had graduated from the RMC. Now, the threat of war and his marriage to my mother gave him the opportunity.

My mother's uncle, married to her father's sister, Aunt Dorothy known as *Doll,* was Colonel Rose Price of the Welsh Guards. Colonel Rose had started the First War serving in the Indian Army in France but had subsequently transferred to the British Army and, because of his Welsh ancestry, had joined the newly formed Welsh Guards. The Regiment had been raised at the time when the British Army needed a million extra men to make up for the losses of the first year of war and its formation was designed to encourage recruiting from the Principality. Its first officers and NCOs were drawn from throughout the other regiments of the Brigade of Guards and in particular from the Grenadiers. It had received its first stand of Colours on St David's Day, the 1st March, 1915.

Colonel Rose's son, Robin, like my father, had initially joined a Regiment of the Line, the Royal Welch Fusiliers, not having sufficient means for the Brigade. Robin heard from his father that the Welsh Guards were planning to recruit additional officers to fill their ranks and were on the lookout for the best that they could obtain. Both Robin and my father made successful applications and, in the autumn of 1939, my father was able to transfer to his new Regiment and become an officer in the Brigade of Guards.

It was generous of Robin, his cousin by marriage, to have tipped off my father in this way because my father had seniority over Robin in the Army List. Robin was to go on to have a distinguished wartime career in the Welsh Guards, commanding its Third Battalion in the Italian campaign and winning the Distinguished Service Order (DSO) for outstanding service.

Some years ago, I went to lunch outside Oxford with Christopher Spence the founder of the Lighthouse charity and was introduced to his father. On hearing my name, Christopher's father said 'Are you any relation of *Johnnie* Fass? '. When I replied that I was his son, he told me that he had been an HAC cadet at Bulford in 1939 and remembered the evening when my father had retired to his room dressed as an immaculately turned out Company Commander of the Royal Berkshire Regiment and had re-appeared the following morning as an even more immaculately turned out Company Commander of the Welsh Guards!

It was the 4th October 1939 and my father wrote to my mother that he was delighted with the change and that he was certain that it was the best thing that he had ever done in his life except one thing - and that was marrying her!

The Training Battalion

On the 1st of January 1940 my father left the OCTU on Salisbury Plain and was posted to the Training Battalion, Welsh Guards at Colchester. His seniority in the new regiment was confirmed in the rank of Captain and his appointment as a Company Commander fully justified his decision to transfer. The Battalion trained both newly joined officers and guardsmen and was commanded by a veteran of the First War, Lord Glanusk. One of his fellow company commanders was Captain David Davies-Scourfield who was to become a particular friend of the family. David was later to command the Third Battalion in North Africa.

My father's service with the Training Battalion marked his formal arrival in the Regiment. Standards were very high and many of the young officers and guardsmen were to remember him for the rest of their war service and some for rest of their lives. Others, like Nigel Fisher, were already known to my father. Nigel was a friend of Michael Verey's from Cambridge who was later to serve as a Squadron Commander in the Regiment's Second (tank) Battalion; go on to win an MC at Nijmegen Bridge and to become an MP after the war.

My father's acquaintance with many of these individuals would be renewed as the war went on. When he was Brigade Major of 33rd Guards Brigade for nine months from December 1941 to August 1942, the Third Battalion, Welsh Guards formed one of its units and in April 1944 he was first a Company Commander and then the Commanding Officer of its First Battalion in Normandy. Many of these individuals wrote to my mother when he was killed saying that my father had taught them much of what they knew about soldiering and that their survival in war was in part due to him. Amongst these as well as Nigel Fisher were Bedingfeld, Dowding, Gibson-Watt, Harmsworth, Koppel, Llewellyn, Miller, Powell, Shepley-Cuthbert, Vaughan, Watt and Worrell a number of whom would serve as his Company Officers in Normandy.

In early 1940 a new wartime battalion, Second Battalion, Welsh Guards was formed and a number of officers who my father had trained whilst commanding a company in the Training Battalion were transferred into it of which Nigel Fisher was one. In 1943 the Second Battalion would be converted into a mechanised tank unit and would fight alongside the Regiment's First Battalion in Normandy commanded by my father as a formation of the Guards Armoured Division. In a letter to my mother, who was not able to attend as she was recovering from flu, my father described the ceremony of the presentation of its Colours by HM King George VI on the 14th February 1940. It was a kind of home-coming for him.

'Oh dear you would have enjoyed it so I do so wish you had been able to come. It was sickening that you could not and I missed having you dreadfully all the other people there with their wives and you could have met some of them. They were not wildly smart as some of those were at the cocktail party we went to at Windsor. It may have been the cold but you would have looked a fair treat in your little fur hat and fur coat.

Well now I arrived to find a great deal of hanging about and congregating. Nigel (Fisher) in very good heart and pleased to see me. Robin (Rose Price) not so but probably rather wound up about all the arrangements and so on (Adjutant to the 2nd Battalion) – in very good form nevertheless. Early on Aunt Doll arrived (my mother's aunt and married to Colonel Rose (one time Colonel of the Regiment) looking extremely smart and nice –blue hat and veil and smart blue coat – endless questions but very sweet and asked tenderly after you and when she heard that you were still in bed said that she would write again to cheer you up! She could not have been nicer but I found her hard to talk to and tended to have little to say.

A place was all arranged for you indoors in the Mess so that you would not have had to sit about in the cold – reserved for special people!

Then we all trooped out and the Companies came on to parade. *Very* good they were and the more so as they were Reservists or young soldiers, The officers also considering that they were mostly wartime soldiers were very good too. Then the King arrived dressed as the Colonel of the WG – looking incredibly young – very well and very sunburnt rather obviously a lamp I thought. He had a marvellous grey overcoat on and looked grand.

Various palavers of *present arms* and general salutes and inspections, etc went on and then the Colours in their waterproof cases were brought on – unrolled and placed on a pile of drums in front of the monarch –the chaplain for the Tower (of London) then came out – dressed in medieval fashion with a well-wadded blue velvet cushion on his head and read an interminably long service which unfortunately is laid down but which in view of the cold could well have been shortened considerably – we stood getting colder and colder – really dreadfully cold and then the Colours were blessed and presented to the Ensigns who were kneeling in front of the drums – all this done by the King.

He then made a very good little speech – its rather awful to *see* him stammering, one can see him fighting to stay calm – he did quite well though except for one word. The CO of the 2nd Battalion then replied in an admirable little speech and then the Colours marched back into the line and all the Bn. then marched past us in 3s. Another Present etc. and then away we went. It was all rather thrilling and one felt rather Cavalcade-ish!

Well then we all trooped into the Mess and there was a great smoothing of hairs and straightening of ties and we got ready to be presented. We came one after another like one does at a levee, – halted in front of him and bobbed our head down – shook him by the hand – bobbed again and went off. I hope I did it all right – I think I did.

My father found his fellow officers in the Brigade a great change from his former regiment. Everyone was charming, fun and interesting compared to the Royal Berkshires although he was anxious that this should not reach their ears! In London he met *Chicko* Leetham, the Colonel Commanding the Regiment who he remarked was 'a typical Guardsman – incredibly tall with typical moustache – seemed very nice' and Dudley-Ward, the Regimental Adjutant. Given his experience as an Instructor at the RMC he was initially made responsible for officer training but soon took over a Company (No. 2) whose training schedule he organised as he had done at the Depot in Reading.

However he was critical of the way that the British Army was responding to the needs of war. There was much chaos and too many both serving and retired officers recalled to the Colours who were not up to date with the latest methods and old fashioned in their opinions. He was also anxious about the way that the recruits drawn from civilian life would respond. He wrote that they were 'really appalling quite unlike guardsmen and really rather poor'. About senior officers Alanbrooke now CIGS wrote later:

> "Half our Corps and Divisional commanders are totally unfit for their appointments and yet if I was to sack them I could find no better! They lack character, imagination, drive and powers of leadership"

and about wartime recruits that:

> "His chest is flat, his stomach unhealthily swollen. There is dandruff lurking in the brilliantine and he carries himself as if he has no shape". (Allport).

His first reference to the war situation came from a friend with whom he had been at the RMC who described the way he thought that the Germans would sweep through Belgium avoiding the Maginot Line and comparing this with the view of the French that Hitler would be defeated by June 1940!

The Lieut-Colonel Commanding the Regiment, was its most senior serving officer and responsible for all things regimental and in particular for its officers. He visited the Battalion and my father raised the matter of the Staff College with him. My father's expectations for attendance in 1938 and 1939 had not been met. It was now 1940 and the country was at war. After nine years of regimental soldiering, the Staff College was becoming my father's principal career goal. The Colonel responded that, of course, my father would wish to look after his own interests, but that he could not be spared at present. My father commented after the meeting with the Colonel that 'they are rather difficult chaps to deal with these fellows delightfully "of course, old boy" and vague and rather hard to pin down definitely to anything'.

On the 1st of March 1940 my father participated in his first Welsh Guards St David's Day celebrations:

'We started off by going for a church service in the NAAFI (canteen) the whole battalion to which the Bishop of Chelmsford came. I've never, never heard such superb singing. Everyone of those guardsmen sang flat out and magnificently at that. The Regimental choir soaring away in parts and the rest all swelling out in unison. They sang the hymns to old Welsh tunes which they all knew and it was incredibly moving even in the mundane atmosphere of the NAAFI and brought tears to the eyes of the Bishop who was a charming individual – the typical prelate with hair brushed rather straight to the side and the general crow- like appearance that Holy men seem to acquire. He preached an admirable sermon and then we all filed out onto parade and marched past Billy Fox Pitt now as you know Brigadier.

Everything went well and after marching past and lining up to present arms we then individually went and got our leek and the 4 Captains took a box of them to distribute to their Companies. After the parade there was wonderful champagne buffet in the Mess-magnificently done and to which extremely nice people came unlike other functions we have been to in the past.'

A month later the matter of the Staff College raised its head again. In a letter to my mother dated 4th April 1940, my father wrote:

'Today is epoch making and one that may alter our while life so pray for success. As you said it was a good thing to have gone and stayed with G (Lt. Col. Greenacre now commanding the Training Battalion) and would appear to have borne fruit already – I may be wrong but this is what happened. Apropos of nothing at all this afternoon at tea he turned to me and said I've been thinking about you and your staff course and don't think that I am even going to recommend you now.

I was duly horrified and the long and short of it was that he told me there and then to make out an application to attend the Staff Course in May sent a covering letter that he typed immediately which said that whilst the Lt. Col. and he had decided not to recommend me until I had been a little longer in the Bn I had done very well whilst I had been down here – that he had someone else whom he could make a Coy. Comm. in my place that I was Regular and therefore had to think of my career and that as I would find it harder to get on a course once I had been sent abroad he thought that if I could get on the staff course it would be a good thing.

Knowing the man it wasn't bad and worth masses of Philip Hight's effusions. He said there was not much time and that therefore I'd better go off and post the letter at once to catch the post!! Rather incredible

He also said what you have said that unless one pushed it no one else would and that he and the Lt. Col. (Leatham) would always try to hang onto me.

George Browning who is quite charming (Lt. Col. George who was later the First Battalion's first commanding officer in Normandy) told me that he is practically certain that my name is already down for the Staff Course as a result of my previous application so that really things look shall I say suddenly rather hopeful. It is quite incredible how something suddenly turns up.

The one snag may be that there are only 20 vacancies about for

Eastern Command which now includes London District and therefore the Brigade whereas in peace had a separate allocation for themselves – any way it's a colossal step forward – I am incredibly elated and it only goes to show.

This of course may change all our plans so we shall have to see....
I feel incredibly bucked about all of this as I hope you will be but don't count on it too much for fear of disappointment.'

Alas, it was not to be. On the 10th April he wrote:

'So soon our hopes have been dashed and shattered I went up to London today to Regimental HQ to try to clinch the Staff Course – they did not much like the idea but consented to ring up Brigade to find out whether I could get on only to be told that only those who had already qualified in Peace were being taken so that I was not eligible as I have not ever sat the exam – rather a bitter disappointment really however they promised that if they could they would get me on the next one.'

There could have been a number of explanations for the passions that had been raised by the continuing saga of the Staff College. First, my father's service in the Welsh Guards was comparatively brief and the Regiment may not yet have been completely confident about my father's qualities although he had made an early good impression. Second, as the Regiment raised its wartime battalions, it was desperately short of experienced officers to train and lead its new recruits. My father was an asset to the Regiment at a critical time and they did not want to lose him. Against that, Leetham and Greenacre were both aware of the need to satisfy the ambitions of a regular officer and may also have been pleased at the prospect of an officer of the Regiment representing them on the Staff in the higher ranks of the Army. Third, from my father's perspective, this was something that he felt that he had earned through his successful career to date some of which had carried with it the usual frustrations of employment and that it would lead to more rapid promotion and to appointments to posts in the higher direction of the war. Finally, there was one other factor that must have played a part and that was that the Staff College would mean that my father and mother could live together for at least the duration of the course which was something that he spoke and wrote about to her on a daily basis.

It was the spring of 1940 and as my father trained his Guardsmen outside London and continued his campaign for entry to the Staff College, the BEF was soon to be thoroughly beaten in France. Both the First and Second Battalions of the Regiment were involved in the campaign and suffered grievously with officers and guardsmen killed and, mainly as a result of their courageous defence of Boulogne, 453 made prisoners. My father wrote 'I still cannot get the 12 officers and 400 men out of my mind and am filled with fury against the Germans and against the politicians etc in this country who have sat back and done so little for the last 8 months'.

Senior Officer School

One consequence of the defeat of BEF was the realisation of the need for more highly skilled leaders at regimental level. Up to that time, each commander made his own plans and tactical dispositions on the battlefield. There was no commonly accepted way to fight a company, a battalion or a brigade. The difficulties this caused had been highlighted by the experience of the BEF and the professional heads of the Army realised that something needed to be done. A senior officers school was created at Erlestoke in Devizies to train future regimental commanders and on the 6th May 1940 my father was one of its first students. This may have been a consolation prize for not going to the Staff College at the time. The job of the School was to prepare officers for commands of battalions and regiments and instil in them some common tactical doctrine.

He was dismayed on his arrival when he found that the camp was a wreck; that he had to sleep in a tent and that the food was revolting. His fellow students were not much better and he described them variously as "dimwits, diehards, deadbeats and dug-outs" the latter being retired officers who had returned to the Colours at the beginning of the war. There were also a number of TA colonels. They all had a lot to say about the running of a war! It was not long before the Army realized that such individuals would be inadequate in a fight and that TA battalions should always be commanded by a regular. He was the youngest on the course by at least ten years and his study syndicate was dominated by a Seaforth officer with foul breath! Half way through the course because of the situation in France, all the commanding officers of battalions were recalled and a number of new students began to arrive who were younger and more fun to be with. The work was hard and the Instructors became more bearable as time went on.

During his time on the course the BEF had been defeated in France. My father wrote:

'No further news about France really – we still don't know what is happening about the French Fleet (it was stationed in North Africa and the Allies were anxious that it might fall into German hands in which case the odds on an invasion would be greatly increased. In the event Prime Minister Churchill ordered that it should be sunk at its moorings – author's note) which is all important but when things begin happening I'm afraid they will happen quick. We must decide what you and Serena must do . I can't have you bombed and machine gunned and treated like French - they apparently materially helped to cause the disorganisation and final rout of the French. I feel the Finnish example (The Finns had been engaged in a war holding off the Russians – author's note) is one that we want to follow'.

On the 24th of June my father completed the course gaining another "Distinguished" on his record. The course report read:

'Captain Fass is an outstanding officer for his age and rank. He has a pleasant manner, a cheerful personality and a keen sense of humour. I judge him to have considerable character and to be a good leader. He is fit to stand up to prolonged physical strain. He has a quick brain full of common sense. His standard of military knowledge is good. I classify him as an officer of marked ability fit for immediate command and likely to be fit for further advancement later, after active service experience. He is also suitable for training for the General Staff.'

There were a number of significant comments in the report. First, the comment about his fitness confirmed the latest Army Order which was that all ranks had to participate in regular "runs". This was one way of getting rid of the "dug outs"; another was that officers had to be under the age of 40 on the 1st January 1940 to be eligible to serve. Second, that he was assessed as fit to command. Shortly afterwards he made reference to this in a letter to my mother about the possibility of commanding one of the new formations that it was proposed should be raised for wartime service as independent units and even thought about the command of a TA battalion.

This almost became a reality because in December 1940 when he was back with the Welsh Guards an officer with whom he had been at the Senior Officers School wrote to him in the following terms:

```
Ist Bn. The Cambridgeshire Regt.
Wymondham
Norfolk
Dear Fass,

I am now commanding this battalion and we have a vacancy
for a Major which we are unable to fill within the unit.
It is absolutely essential that we have a regular officer
and there is no one available from the Suffolk Regiment
which is our affiliated regiment.
Our Div. Commander is Major Gen. Beckwith Smith who you
no doubt know but even if you do not know him it occurred
to him that there might be somebody in the Brigade of
Guards who we might be able to get to fill this. I do not
know how you are situated and no doubt you are probably
a temporary Major by now in one of your own Bns. If you
are in any way stuck I thought you might possibly like to
come here as I am sure we would get on very well together
and you would rank as second Senior Major in the Bn. And
I think your future would be very rosy.
When I was asked if I knew anybody in the Bde. of Guards
who might possibly be able to come I mentioned your  name
to the Div. Comdr and I think he is accordingly asking if
you are available.
Of course you may well not want to leave the Bde. of
Guards but  I feel sure if you felt there was promotion
going outside which would suit  you, you would be very
happy here
```

```
Please let me know by return what your views are,

Yours sincerely

GG Carpenter

This is a T/A Bn.  Men and NCOs selected — training
backward.  Officers trainable, but will be adjusted! Now
starting Bren gun carrier Trg. And I think we shall be
very good if we are allowed to finish it.'
```

This was a tempting offer as my father was becoming increasingly frustrated at the way that his application for the Staff College was being delayed. He remained in the rank of Captain and observed others either of lesser ability (in his estimation), of lower rank to himself or holding war time commissions officers being promoted above him.

The Cambridgeshire Regiment was one of only two in the British Army (the other was the Herefordshire Regiment) which was a volunteer regiment with no regular troops. In the event the Regiment was posted to the Far East and its soldiers were either killed or captured at the fall of Singapore and suffered the dreadful privations of imprisonment by the Japanese.

Finally in the report, the comment about the idea of active service experience being necessary for advancement compared to the reference to the Staff continued to annoy my father. The tension that it had created over the previous three years would, I believe, have continued to have a profound influence upon the rest of his career and up to the time of his death.

By the beginning of June 1940 the British Army had been defeated at Dunkirk and more news began to reach England of the grievous losses that had been incurred. My mother wrote to my father on Jun 4th:

'Well, now we know 335,000 returned and 30,000 killed, wounded or missing. I don't think it's too bad really, do you? It sounds a lot but probably there are not more than 10,000 dead out of that 30,000 and that is bearable...what was the name of that Cadet of yours in the Guards, that we saw dancing at Quags (Quaglino's) with his wife both tall and fair, do you remember – he was just married. Was it Arthur Boyd because I see that he has been killed – I do hope it wasn't they looked so pathetic, do you remember? I was talking to a woman in the village today, waiting for Ma outside the schools and a woman with a pram and husband (in grey flannels) passed on the other side. The woman called out "How are you Frank?" and Frank bright red and grinning said "All right now thank you – better than I was 2 days ago". Two days ago he was lying on Dunkirk beach!! Did your mother tell you that John and Peter (the Wrightson boys) and Desmond (Magill) are all back. Peter lay for 2 days on the beach with his face in the sand and shells busting all around. Can you imagine it......the Berks have had a thin time of it and are much cut up.'

Great Britain and its Commonwealth allies now stood alone against the Axis Powers that included Italy, despite that country having been our ally in the First Great War. America was at best neutral and indifferent and at worst positively hostile and Japan was soon to threaten the East. By the early autumn of 1940 invasion had become a very real possibility if the German Luftwaffe could defeat the fighter aircraft of the Royal Air Force in the skies above the South of England. Hitler ordered the preparation of landing craft for a sea crossing at the newly captured port of Boulogne. France had surrendered. My mother and father spoke about their own evacuation plans for the family possibly to Canada but more likely to Dacre or Dalemain in Cumberland where my mother and Serena could stay with her family's Hasell relatives and be kept out of harm's way.

In a letter to his father in law, Henry Verey, my father wrote an *appreciation* of what he thought was the situation:

'1. Hitler will attempt to invade us, may have some small measure of success initially and will undoubtedly try in several places at once, possibly from Ireland amongst others.
2. That we shall be bombed and possibly gassed.
3. That if nothing worse it will be all most unpleasant.'

At the beginning of the war, Henry Verey had asked my father what he

96

considered would be the fate of Henry's two sons, Philip and Michael, and of himself, all of whom would be serving in the Army. My father had responded by saying that Philip, serving in a relatively poor quality TA Battalion would be unlikely to ever see a shot fired in anger; that Michael serving in a horse-mounted yeomanry regiment would not fight for at least two years when it had been fully mechanised and that as for himself, he would, most probably, be dead within the next two weeks! When this was reported to Henry's wife and the two brothers, great offence was taken! However, his assessment was quite correct.

As it turned out my mother did not go to Cumberland but went to stay at Bridge House with her parents (Mapletons having been returned to its owner Lord Iliffe) whilst making trips up to London to meet my father whenever possible, sometimes in his mother's flat at 22, Cranmer Court. Likewise, my father came down to Twyford on short weekend leaves when he could. Trains were delayed or cancelled, roads blocked and telephone lines were down due to the bombing so it was not an easy time to move about. They wrote to each other every day but saw each other infrequently and it was a very frustrating time. However, in August 1940 just as the Blitz was starting, they took a flat close to where my father was stationed so they could spend time with each other occasionally.

On 18th September 1940 eight months pregnant with their second child and the baby due a month later, my mother was informed that the child she was expecting would be stillborn. She then had to go through the agonies of giving birth and was very unwell afterwards. They were both devastated by this event which was so unexpected and near to term. My father was given one week's compassionate leave which they spent in the comparative calm of my mother's grandmother's family home at Dalemain in Cumberland.

The First Battalion & the Blitz

On his return to regimental duty he was posted to the First Battalion at Elstree in Hertfordshire lately returned from France. He commented 'they (the Company) only came back 22 strong from France so that one had to start from scratch'. He was a little anxious that because the battalion had been together for so long and through such troubles that he would feel excluded from their society but he settled in quickly and

97

found some old friends amongst the officers although he did not approve of all of them. He felt that a number of the wartime intake were too showy and loud and not at all what might be expected in the Brigade and in comparison to the pre-war army. Although he was delighted to hear that Nigel Fisher had been promoted to Captain and made second in command of a company in the Second Battalion, he bridled at the idea of Nigel knowing his military business sufficiently after one and a half years in uniform compared to his own service of nine and a half years. He was also unhappy that Nigel would now receive the same pay as him at 16/6 per day (c. 80p). When he reviewed the work of the Battalion he felt that although the Guardsmen were magnificent he did not rate their chances in the event of invasion: they were simply insufficiently prepared, trained and equipped.

By September the RAF had beaten off the Luftwaffe from above its airfields and the Germans had changed their tactics. Using the line of the silvery Thames they began to carry out large scale bombing raids on London by night and on other major industrial centres. The Blitz had begun. The First Battalion stationed on the outskirts of London was soon in the thick of it and on the 12th September 1940 my father reported:

'We were called out to make a cordon round the burnt and bruised area by St Pauls. Later, enter an excited CSM (Company Sergeant Major) to say that the Company had to move in 15 mins to go and fight a fire and keep crowds away. So all helter skelter and swearing and off in 20 mins. Whenever we came to a block - and there were many - we merely drove on the wrong side of the road and hooted loudly. They had tried to bomb all the bridges and in every case the bombs had fallen on the northern bank, never more than 200 yards away. Big bombs too. The Kings Road had a lot. Past St Thomas's Hospital and then we got onto the scene of the fire which was considerable but really made little difference to the trend of the war. 3 large bombs again arrived at the bridges which had caused a fire which had spread more than was necessary because all the firemen were elsewhere fighting other fires. They had a lot of difficulty getting it under control. The firemen were superb and in great spirits although they had been on the job for 72 hours. The rescue squads grand – funny little dirty men – grand cockneys –

"look out, Sir" and a whole lot of flares would come hurtling down. The "Citz" (citizens) very good too – all joking about non-existent businesses and very few depressed and non-defeatist – I thought they were superb. We had Winston (Winston Churchill, the Prime Minister) - although I gave him of my best in the way of salutes he unfortunately got out at my Company HQ when I was away. The GOC (General Officer Commanding) London District and Uncle Rose (Col. Rose Price) Often I was surprised at the amount of bits of London that had been hit.'

In a subsequent letter to my mother he wrote

'We confidently expect invasion any day now – personally I think that though it may be tried, like the invincible armada the Navy and Air Force will never allow it to get near the coast. The barrage was not so intense last night that we had a comparatively quiet night last night I'm glad to say tho' the brute Hitler does seem to have knocked London about a bit. I have not seen any of it only the pictures in the papers of the end of the Burlington Arcade and Regent Street. Naturally the papers make the worst of it and take the most shattered vistas – the surprising thing is how calm and untroubled by it all everyone seems to be and as the papers say the only thoughts are those of hate against Hitler. I personally am beginning to expect London to be laid flat. Tell Papa (Henry Verey) that he should get from Morland (the gardener) about 12 sandbags, fill them with sand and ½ a bag does a bomb (incendiary) – you can hear them whistle as they come down and if one did fall on the roof it might be tiresome as one might never know it was there'.

In a letter to Michael Verey, his brother in law and by now in the Middle East, he wrote:

'Incidentally the bombing is nothing like as bad as you would guess from the newspapers – mind you a sort of toothless look here and there but most of it is still there. We have visitations from time to time which once sent me under my bed but none of us have ever been in a shelter nor any of my Guardsmen'.

After the report from the Senior Officers School had been delivered, he made his third and final assault on the Staff College. The new Commanding Officer of the First Battalion, Julian Jefferson, remarked that WM and my father 'were the only two Company Commanders who were able to train companies' but agreed that he should go in January 1941 although he added that 'they were short of good people and that if I went on the Staff I would be away for the war, etc etc'. Leatham continued to prevaricate and had to be reminded that it was a promise that had been made to my father when he had transferred to the Regiment.

Although Jefferson had written on his application 'an officer of outstanding ability who is well suited to be a SO (staff officer) Instructional ability well above the average' the Regimental Adjutant, Charles Dudley-Ward, remained unhappy and wrote to my father in the following terms:

Dear Johnny'

Your name remains on the list for the Junior Staff Course but I want to put on record now the warnings I gave you over the phone.

The impression — and I may say it is more than an impression, it is a fact — that remains from your efforts to follow your ambition in that you place your own advancement before the good of your Regiment. This, you may say, is harsh, but you know very well the effect of the continual expansion of the Regiment and that we have not a sufficient number of officers capable of commanding and training a Company — we are, and you know it, struggling against almost insuperable difficulties. It is no use pretending that one year's experience in the Army is as good as ten years and our weak position in number of trained officers must effect the Service Battalions in action.

I also take the view that no officer who has the opportunity of going into action in command of troops should miss it, no matter what he may have to forego in order to do so. An officer of your age should, in my opinion, put all else aside in order to command his company in action- it must be an experience of the greatest value which no soldier with staff ambitions should miss.

However, there it is, Johnny. You will go through this
Staff course, disappear from your regiment for the rest
of the war and never know anything of the handling of
a company in action — quite a common situation amongst
staff officers but none the less the curse of our Army
system,

You may say that your Regiment does nothing for you but
the whole existence of the Army is based on service given
not on favours received.

My father's response to this hurtful response to his legitimate desire
for advancement showed the deep frustration that the affair of the Staff
College had caused him and my mother thought that Charles was an old
bore:

Dear Charles, Your views on if and when officers should
go to the Staff College is an entirely separate question.
In my opinion your criticisms are neither fair nor
just. Among other things in identical circumstances qua
the Regiment, another officer with similar service and
experience has been recommended although not previously
even on the Staff College list. When I joined the
Regiment I was told by the Colonel (Fox-Pitt) that my
doing so should not prejudice in any way my going to the
Staff College and that this step would not be delayed.
Further, I understood from the Lieutenant-Colonel when
I saw him in August that he agreed that my name should
be put up for this Course, and that as a result of his
telephone conversation with Colonel Johnson if I did not
go on this course in September I should probably go in
January.' It is reasonable to expect that promises once
given will be adhered to.

This correspondence showed the tension on which my father had already
remarked in his career between the foundation of the Army's military
virtues which was the Regimental system based on loyalty and tradition
compared to the intellectual challenges of the Staff with its more varied
prospects

This dilemma continued to influence the remainder of my father's life.
Three years later in 1944 he was in a very senior position on the Staff
with the prospect of further promotion when COSSAC, the planning

staff before D-Day, became the SHAEF (Supreme Allied Headquarters Allied Expeditionary Force) staff just prior to the Invasion. He might well have remained there where his work was highly regarded by his superiors and also because they had doubts about the wisdom of him serving in the front line when he had critical Intelligence in his head about future Allied operational plans. It would have been disastrous for him to have fallen into the enemy's hands.

However, he had chosen a career as a soldier and I believe that he could not have imagined himself going through the whole of the war as a staff officer and without having the experience of command in battle. As my father crossed to France in June 1944 Dudley Ward's words would be proved to have been profoundly wrong.

Chapter Eight
STAFF OFFICER

Staff College

Finally, at the age of 29 and after nine and a half years service, my father was on his way professionally again when he joined the Staff College at Camberley on 18th January 1941.

The pre-war Staff College course had lasted two years, during which students had absorbed not only every aspect of staff duties but also learned about new developments in strategic and tactical thinking and made connections that would last them throughout their careers. In war time the emphasis changed to turning out the largest number of competent staff officers who would subsequently hold the expanding number of staff jobs in brigades, divisions and higher formations. The course was shortened to five months and focussed on the essentials of staff work. .

There is very little to record of his time at Camberley. All that can be surmised is that he had never worked harder in his life. The hours were long and the Instructors hard. These were drawn from amongst the cleverest men in the army and with vast experience of its innermost workings. Students were placed in syndicates for their work and they had to master every detail of all the arms and branches of the service from guns and tanks to pay and bedrolls. The course included inter-service cases involving the Royal Navy and the RAF and this would be helpful when my father joined the COSSAC staff and was responsible, amongst other activities, for liaison with other formations and services.

Syndicates were given puzzles to solve: How to get a Division across a river or desert, how to plan the firing orders of a battery of guns or how to repel a gas attack. Many of the case studies were based on actual examples of warfare, for example, Allenby's campaign in the Middle East in the First World War. Each student's work was marked and commented on by the Directing Staff (DS) and syndicates also made group presentations. My father and his RMC Instructor friend Bernard Fergusson of the Black Watch were in the same syndicate and often made joint presentations.

In whatever spare time he had available he dedicated himself to his favourite sport, hunting, where he was the joint Master of the Staff College Draghounds, the oldest pack of draghounds in the country. At the end of the course in May 1941 both he and Fergusson passed out A1, the highest mark possible for the course, and were able to put the coveted letters *PSC* or Passed Staff College after their names on the Army List.

Brigade Major – 225th Brigade

The most sought after appointment on graduation as a staff officer was to be appointed as Brigade Major to a Brigade of the Field Army. To have been a successful Assistant and Acting Adjutant of an infantry battalion; the Adjutant of a regimental depot and an instructor at the RMC was one thing, but for a newly minted graduate of the Staff College to be appointed Brigade Major was something else altogether! Brigade majors were famously meticulous in their attention to the smallest detail, serious about all matters military and relentless in their pursuit of excellence. Only two members of his course of c. 50 students attained this appointment immediately on leaving the Staff College. The Brigade Major was the chief of staff to the Brigade Commander, the Brigadier, and was responsible for executing not only his orders but also for responding to his every whim. The Brigade Major acted as the link, and stood as the buffer between, its commander and the regiments and corps of the Brigade which in an infantry brigade usually consisted of three front- line battalions with their supporting arms of gunners, engineers, medics, transport, etc.

His initial appointment was as Brigade Major to 225th Brigade whose headquarters was at Wooler in Northumberland and whose area of responsibility was the north Northumberland coastline and its interior. The task of Home Forces, of which the Brigade was a part, was twofold. First, it was to defend the country against what was still thought of at the time as the very real possibility of a German invasion in the summer of 1941. Second, it was to train its units up to a standard that would enable them to be used offensively in overseas theatres of war. Whilst this appointment may have been far from London or Twyford, he was on familiar ground as he and his Yorkshire cousins, the Wrightsons, had many connections with the area and in particular with a number of the County families that included those of Collingwood, Lambton, Reed, Pease, Sale, Straker-Smith, and de Stein, the latter the owners of Lindisfarne castle.

The Brigade was commanded by Brigadier James Pendlebury of the East Lancashire Regiment who had won a Military Cross (MC) as a young officer in Flanders during the First World War and a Distinguished Service Order (DSO) whilst in command of its First Battalion in France in 1940. The Brigade consisted of three Territorial battalions the 10th Kings Royal Regiment (Lancaster); the 9th Border Regiment (Cumbria) and the 12th Kings Regiment (Liverpool). These were each regiments of the Territorial Army that were led by a small number of senior officers and NCOs and were in the process of being brought up to strength by drafts of retired regulars returning to the Colours, pre-war TA soldiers now serving on a full time basis and newly recruited wartime volunteers. These troops were keen but virtually untrained and their officers suffered the same shortcomings as my father had experienced with their like on the War Course in 1940. He remarked that the Brigade: 'needs a damn good clean out of the hopeless ones' but that the north country soldiers of the Brigade were '100% kinder, less grumbly and talk to you as equals and yet never take advantage in any way, far nicer that the Berks or the Welsh if it comes to it.' He was not pleased, however, when during a night exercise 'We were raided on a tiresome scheme on Friday and my blue hat was stolen (I've got it back now) but so childish and quite hopeless – I despair of the British Army I think they go beyond words in hopelessness.'

His first impression of the area and his fellow soldiers was not auspicious. A car was waiting for him at Wooler railway station with 'quite the dirtiest driver I had ever seen.' He thought the place (Belford) where Brigade Headquarters was situated was the end 'with dour stone houses and Scottish-type pubs'. The Brigade mess was in a hotel that had been commandeered by the Army and the mess contained three armchairs, a table and a rug! He thought that the Brigadier seemed efficient, kind and easy to get along with. His predecessor left the morning after he arrived so that there could be no handover of duties but he had known the Motor Transport (MT) officer when he had been stationed at Folkestone in the 1930s. One piece of good news was that the Divisional Commander was Major General Money who had been the Commandant of the Senior Officers School when my father had attended it in 1940.

However, he soon found ways to get out and about and enjoyed the Northumberland countryside as he visited the battalions and their defences 'The country is lovely and the people far, far nicer than in the South.'

My father was not only familiar with the divisional commander Money, who had been Commandant of the Senior Officers School, but also with the C-in-C, Northern Command Lieut-General Eastwood, originally of the Rifle Brigade, who had been Commandant of the Royal Military College at Sandhurst when my father had been an instructor there in 1939. Shortly after my father had arrived at 225th Brigade, Eastwood brought General Alanbrooke, the Commander in Chief Home Forces, to visit the Brigade. Brooke was soon to be appointed by Prime Minister Winston Churchill the CIGS and Chairman of the Joint Chiefs of Staff, responsible for the military conduct of the war. My father reported:

'The C in C Brook I was only fairly impressed with but though he came up to see us all he really looked at nothing and did not allow himself the time to do so. Rather asked questions but didn't really listen when they were answered. Fairly prepossessing but talked quickly and should not have said was a great brain. He shook me warmly by the hand and asked me how I had enjoyed the Staff Course (College). *Rusty* Eastwood was effusive. Saw me immediately came over and wrung me by the hand like a long lost friend, talked for a long time and I was rather a *king-pin* among the extremely dim others for knowing him. Money also fairly cordial but nothing like as much as Rusty E. Far more looking after his own thunder. Rusty came down again today and greeted me with "Hello old boy" and Money was more cordial. I was really more impressed by Rusty and his grasp of the situation than by Brook.'

Alanbrooke wrote in his diary about the visit:

28 May

Left here at 8.00am, took off from Hendon in the Airspeed Envoy at 8.45am. Very cloudy and flying at 3000ft never saw the floor. Reached Newcastle at 10.20am where I was met by Eastwood, who had just taken over from Adam (Northern Command), also Robin Money. We then toured Northumberland coast up to just short of Bamburgh Castle. Finally took off from Acklinton at 6.45 and did not reach Hendon till 8.45pm. The defences of Northumberland are certainly alarmingly thin. But then the more I go around the coast the more I realise how desperately thin our defences are' (Alanbrooke, in Danchev & Todman).

My father was being somewhat unfair to Brooke who had more important things on his mind at the time, not least the developing situation on the island of Crete and later in the war came to admire him greatly. However, this meeting with some of the great and good of the British Army was extremely significant for my father's future career. It was a part of the jigsaw that was to lead him to COSSAC and his appointment as a D-Day planner. Eastwood had served as Chief of Staff at Gort's Headquarters of the BEF in France and Jock Whitefoord had been on his intelligence staff. Eastwood was appointed C-in-C 8th Corps District /Northern Command and Jock was his BGS (Brigadier General Staff). After one further appointment as a brigade major in the South of England, my father returned to 8th Corps District and worked for Jock as a GSO2 (general staff officer). When Jock was appointed the first Head of Intelligence and promoted to Major General at COSSAC in early 1943 he took my father with him from 8th Corps/Northern Command to London as his GSO 1 (Operations and Intelligence Liaison) in the rank of Lieutenant-Colonel. The puzzle about the way that my father was appointed to COSSAC was now solved!

It was Jock Whitefoord who had quite literally saved the British Expeditionary Force (BEF) in May 1940 when he advised that a map that had been captured from the overturned and shot-up car of a German staff officer was not a fake but genuine and showed the way that the German Army would attack through Belgium. As a result, early on the morning of 26th May, Lord Gort, the Commander in Chief of the BEF, ordered a general retreat to the coast without obtaining the prior authorisation of the War Cabinet. By the time Churchill was awake it was too late to reverse the order and in consequence the BEF was saved by evacuation across the beaches at Dunkirk. Jock had been an Intelligence Officer on the Western Front in WWI, was a fluent German speaker and had been the British Army's principal liaison officer with Polish Intelligence in London at the beginning of WW2.

My father soon settled into the busy life of a brigade major. There were endless duties to be organised in a formation most of whose members had little previous military experience and he commented that he was run off his feet 'with telephones ringing at every hand and every minute – however I am enjoying it all and get on fine with the Brigadier and with the officers in the Brigade.' He wrote daily to my mother about the glories of the Northumberland countryside and on the vexatious topic of how he was going to find her lodgings locally so that they could be together. She was able to join him for a short time at the end of June 1941 when she stayed with Claud and Olive Lambton at West Newton outside Wooler and in October at Betty Dixon's B& B in Bamburgh with Serena. Betty was well known to the Wrightson family.

Claudie Lambton was the youngest son of the 4th Earl of Durham and had fought in the Grenadiers in the First World War. He had placed a notice in the Brigade's Officers Mess that any officer who wished for a place for his family to stay should contact him. My father did so and Claud and Olive became good friends. When I was young my mother and I used to go up to stay with him in April each year where he taught me to drive his ancient Land Rover and to shoot rabbits sitting in the spare tyre on its bonnet while he drove it erratically over his high sheep pastures!

My father fished for trout in the Borders rivers of his friends and acquaintances; caught his first ever salmon on the Tweed and was even able to arrange for some of his catch to be sent down to my mother at Twyford. Inevitably he found a horse to ride out before breakfast each morning in the company of his beloved dog *Dinty* at his side. He summarily dismissed his Welsh Guards soldier servant and returned him to regimental duty when he discovered that 'I came down before breakfast to tell him something and there he was with his boots off and his feet in a pair of my best brown socks'!

There was a cricket match between the officers and the rest at which he excelled himself:

'You have never seen such duffers – I arrived half way through to find 6 officers out in 5 mins!! Proceeded to make a pretty 21 after being missed several times by people who tumbled over themselves trying to catch my shots. I then proceeded to bowl because no one else could and got two wickets – so "shades of old school" I was duly gratified.'

There were times when he found his military duties frustrating in a brigade-majorish kind of way: 'I've suddenly realised (though I've known it and not had time to do much about it) how desperately inefficient everything is in this HQ and how that no one knows their job properly or does it to any great extent. One *longs* for the Regular Army lazy though it was when people did at least know what they were about.' At the end of July Brigade HQ moved from Wooler to Stocksfield and my father found the move unsettling 'this Mess is appalling! Food dreadful and no organisation or comfort anywhere. Brigadier getting furious in consequence!' It did not help that my mother had addressed a telegram to him c/o Stockfield instead of to the Brigade's military post office number and my father was anxious that he would be in trouble with the Security Police!

His duties were varied as the War Diary of 225th Brigade records during his tour of duty::

26/05/41
11.15 Major J E Fass, the Welsh Guards

```
arrived at this HQ to assume the duties of BM (Brigade
```
Major).
```
28/05/41
11.15 Gen. Sir Ala Brooke KCB, DSO, C in C Home Forces
met commanders of this Brigade at Swinhoe Crossroads
```
(see above for JEF account of visit).
```
29/05/41
Maj Gen T R Eastwood CB, DSO, MC visited Brigade HQ
```
(see above JEF account of visit).
```
30/05/41
Major Fass (BM) carried out a recce of roads
which will be cratered should an emergency
arise.
```

Exercises meant that my father was busy 'Here is a poor man almost in bedlam – we go out on the scheme tomorrow – the telephone never seems to stop ringing – there seems to be 201 things to do and not enough minutes to do them in – everyone very willing but never thinking for themselves because they don't know enough. Up at the crack of dawn tomorrow- what the army calls 0500 hours however like all amateur theatricals, which is more or less what these things are, everything I daresay will be all right on the day.' He reported later in the week 'Got back from the scheme late on Sunday – a fair success only – these boys did rather moderately and today I have just spent my time delivering rockets and therefore everyone is in rather a bad humour. I yearn for one other regular soldier – these people have really little idea of how to go on at all.' When the exercise was over, my father and his brigadier went to a conference in York to be de-briefed. My father reported 'Rusty Eastwood was the big noise and very good indeed and surprisingly dealt out some first rate rockets to high up people like Corps and Divisional Commanders. It was rather fun to be able to sit back and listen and know that by no possible chance whatever could one be brought into trouble.'

A typical exercise involved the Brigade defending the area against a German invasion from the sea.
This required my father to make detailed plans for its disposition. The Orders that he wrote included:

Intention: The Brigade will prevent the enemy
establishing himself on the coast between Crastor and
Redshin Cove.
The troops to be deployed will be 10 King's Own Royal, 9
Border and 12 The King's Regt.
Additional troops will include 61 Field Regt. RA, 269
Anti-tank battalion RA, 59 Div. Recce. Batt., 510 Field
Coy. RE, "D" Coy. RNF (Royal Northumberland Fusiliers), 210
Med. Ambulance.
RAF beach bombing targets
Action against parachute landings
Railway and Police communications
"Stand to":
-Enemy seaborne landings
-Enemy airborne landings
-Use of gas by the enemy
-Identification of POWs (prisoners of war)
-Unexploded bombs
-Presence of mines, depth charges and torpedoes
-"Hot Water" was code name for arrival by enemy by
surface vessel
01/08/41
225 Infantry Brigade moved from Berwick-Wooler-Embleton
to Bynell Hall-Haydon Bridge-Gynnerton-Prudhoe (Tyne
Valley)
18/09/41
Exercise "Pendle" on the line of the River Wansbeck, 20
miles N of the Tyne
Exercise "Hadrian" against enemy forces in and around
Carlisle
13/09/41
Coastguard reported large enemy seaplane landing in the
sea between Berwick on Tweed and St Abbs Head. No further
information could be obtained from the Police or Division
(This may have been the weekend when church bells were rung across
SE England that had been agreed would be the signal that the Germans
had landed)
23/09/41
Soldier and civilian acting in suspicious manner at Beal.
Civilian handed over to the Police. Soldier proved to
be a deserter from the Ox & Bucks LI and was taken into
military custody

My father's initials appear in the bottom right hand corner of many of these Orders for which he was responsible as Brigade Major..

By October 1941 after almost five months in post my father felt that he was now on top of his job but began to hear rumours of change which always unsettled him 'There are still rumours which may mean my going back to other places but nothing definite of any sort' Four days later on the 27th October he wrote;

> 'The bottom has fallen out of my little world – my house has come tumbling about my ears like a pack of cards. That which nearly was when you were up here and that I thought was over and done with has happened. How very disappointed I am and how I shall hate having to leave it all and start somewhere anew – 5 months work as it were wasted and I have never worked so hard to make a success of it and I do honestly believe that things are quite good and are coming along nicely.'

The War Diary records on 1st November 1941:

```
Brig. Pendlebury to 140 Inf. Brigade
Major J E Fass to 33 Ind. Inf. Bde. (Guards)
```

I wonder what had caused his disappointment? Was it because he just hated change or had he other prospects in mind; perhaps the command of one of the battalions of the Brigade or an appointment on the Staff of Northern Command under Eastwood? However, all was not lost. Three days later on the 30th October whilst eagerly awaiting news of the impending birth of his second child due on the 7th November, my father wrote:

> 'I am lucky aren't I to get a Guards Brigade much nearer home - must be I should say as a complete shot in the dark – Hounslow...... I don't know the number or anything and only found out that it was a Guards Brigade by ringing London. I shall be honestly sorry to leave here – one is lucky not to have to stay the full time but the regiments are very easy and very pleasant – the country superb, however I am very thrilled.'

This first appointment on the Staff had clearly been a success. My father had been fortunate both in his brigadier and in the troops involved who, whilst they may not have been the most soldierly, had made up for it by their friendliness and willingness to learn. Time off in the Northumberland countryside with all its social and sporting opportunities had been a bonus. The only serious drawback had been that he had seen his wife three times in the past six months. He now faced a very different challenge in the South of England..

Brigade Major – 33rd Guards Brigade

In November 1941 after six months in the North, my father was selected for the prestigious position of Brigade Major to the 33rd Guards Brigade. The Brigade was stationed outside of London at Hatch End (Pinner) and was responsible for the defence of London.

This Brigade was made up of very different military and social material to that of 225th Brigade and contained the cream of the wartime Household Division including 6th Battalion Coldstream Guards, 3rd Irish Guards and 3rd Welsh Guards.

It was Major Sainthill of the Coldstream who, when ordered to surrender to the Germans at Tobruk, replied: "Surrender is not an operation that the Battalion has practised in peacetime and we do not intend to start now" before fighting his way out of the siege. Joe Vandeleur of the Irish Guards who, when he had explained his Battalion's orders for the following day's attack in Normandy, responded to a questioner who said that they would all be killed by remarking "But that is what the Irish Guards are for!"

Cousin Robin Rose Price was serving as a Company Commander in the newly formed 3rd Welsh Guards and would go on to command in the North African and Italian campaigns ending the war as its Commanding Officer in Austria.

Lieut-Colonel J.O. E. *Joe* Vandeleur, who was to become a close family friend, and one of my godfathers, commanded the 3rd Battalion, Irish Guards. My father and Joe had first met in the Middle East when my father was serving in Palestine and took time out with the Sudanese

Camel Corps to which Joe had been seconded. Joe was the first officer of the post-WWI British Army to hold a private Pilot's Licence and had been a popular Adjutant of the 1st Irish Guards in London in the mid-1930s. He was made famous in *Operation Market Garden* in September 1944 and in the film *A Bridge Too Far*, when his Irish Guards battle group of infantry and tanks vainly attempted to reach the defenders of the third of the three bridges at Arnhem held by British paratroopers. Joe was also the last personal friend and brother officer to see my father alive when he visited the 1st Welsh Guards Battalion Headquarters on the morning of my father's death. His wife Veronica was a close friend of my mother's. My mother reported that my father always used to say that Joe's 3rd Battalion, Irish Guards was the smartest and most efficient in the Household Division and under Joe's leadership was to fight with great distinction throughout the Normandy campaign.

My father's first cousin, Oliver *Nod* Wrightson would later serve in Normandy in the 6th Battalion Coldstream Guards where he was present at Brigade Headquarters in the middle of the night of June 30th when the news of my father's death came through on the wireless. It is also likely that it was here that my father first met Major Horrie Noble who had served in the Scots Guards shortly after the end of the First Great War and who had rejoined the Colours aged 40 at the beginning of the Second. In peacetime Horrie was a stockbroker at Hoare & Co., an outstanding sportsman and brilliant real tennis player. He acted as the Brigade's machine gun officer and also became a close family friend and another godfather. He wrote to my mother on my father's death offering to support both her and me. I remember him as always very generous and accompanying us to the Fourth of June and St Andrew's Day celebrations as well as organising surprise river expeditions on the Thames during the summer holidays when he hired a motor cruiser from Messum's boatyard at Bray.

My father travelled down to London where he was looking forward to being nearer to his wife and family. Elizabeth was expecting another child and they were anxious about the birth following the disaster of the previous year. Whilst they had speculated about having a boy, they were delighted when my sister Ginny, originally to be named Victoria, was born on the 17th November 1941 delivered by the faithful family doctor,

Dr.Bird. My parents sent a telegram to Michael Verey serving in the Middle East that read: 'Many thanks wire error of sex compensated by production of second undoubted glamour girl Virginia Anne Elizabeth'. There was to be no Michael John for almost another three years!

At first my mother stayed at Bridge House with her parents whilst she nursed Ginny and visited my father when she could but later they found a house to rent at Hatch End (The End House) and set up home temporarily together.

The commander of 33rd Guards Brigade was Brigadier Julian Jefferson, lately of the Welsh Guards. They knew each other already as Jefferson had commanded the First Battalion in which my father had served as one of its company commanders and Jefferson had recommended my father for the Staff College a year earlier in late 1940. Jefferson had clearly had his eye on my father since that time as earlier in the year my father had written to my mother from Northumberland 'What a strain to have to keep up to scratch for JJ'. Unfortunately between the time of my father's leaving the Battalion in January 1941 and arriving at 33rd Brigade in October 1941, Jefferson had undergone a personality change and had become a thoroughly difficult individual to deal with. Whether it was the arrogance of command, an excess or lack of confidence or something more personal, my father experienced the unhappiest time of the whole of his service in the Army.

My father's Staff Captain was Rowley Errington, later the Earl of Cromer, Governor of the Bank of England and HM Ambassador to the United States, whose newly wedded wife Esme wrote of being invited to dine with Jefferson and his formidable wife Barbara:

```
The most terrifying personage I was ever to meet was
Rowley's then-commander, Brigadier Julian Jefferson:
gruff when he was not silent. We were invited to dine
with him and his even-more commanding wife. Intimidated
by the brigadier's reputation as a stern martinet, the
reality was worse. We sat mainly in an embarrassed
silence, just the four of us, with no third party to ease
the discomfort. Never was such an alarming evening to be
experienced again. Also, I assumed that all senior army
officers were equally blunt and forbidding and decided
```

to avoid them at all costs whenever possible in the
future...........Brigadier Jefferson was barely heard of
again (Cromer).

My mother used to say that Rowley was very much relieved when my
father took over as Brigade Major as his predecessor had been a stuffy
major of the Grenadiers who, unlike my father, had not allowed his
junior staff to take their jackets off in the office during a period of very
hot weather earlier in the year!

The Brigade was a new formation composed mainly of war time service
officers and guardsmen so that training was a priority for all of its
units.

The Brigade's War Diary for the period records the following
activities:

```
30/11/41
Commanding officers
AM Bankier 3WG
JOE Vandeleur 3IG
WS Stewart Bunty Brown 6CG
06/01/42
Exercise "Lightning" (signals) around Luton
In the event of invasion
Orders
Attacking immediately any parachutists Brigade HQ at
Pinner &/or Hayes in the event of failure of normal
banking facilities
Casualties evacuation
Under command: Guards Armoured training wing and Guards
Armoured Car detachment (Royal Family protection)
24/01/42
Airborne attack on Northolt aerodrome likely
Orders
33rd Guards Bde will destroy any enemy threatening
Northolt or HQ Coastak
Command
```

Under command: 142 Field Regt. RA, 384 Battery RA, 506
Battery RA, 562 Field Coy. RE, RASC 32 Gds. Bde.
 April 1942
Exercise "Dragon"; "Python" (testing a move through
London); "Rommel" (anti invasion); "Sapper" (defence
against invasion West Wycombe)
20/05/42
Live firing exercise on Exmoor
8/06/42
Exercise "Pelican" set by 8 Corps
01/08/42
Exercise "Luton" (Portsmouth and Southampton areas
captured by Germans)
11/09/42
Exercise "Air" (to practice marching troops attacked by
aircraft) 15/09/42
Exercise "Adder" (approx one month of exercises)

As Brigade Major he was obliged to act as the buffer between the Brigade commander's temperament and its regimental leaders and to mitigate the worst aspects of his personality and command style. This he achieved in exemplary fashion as those who knew him testified when he left the Brigade on promotion nine months later in August 1942. In a farewell letter Rowley Errington, who worked for him in his office wrote:

'Saying goodbye is always odious and you know just how sorry I was to see you go. We miss you very much already and I think we will miss you more and more. I myself miss you very badly as our partnership from my point of view was a very happy one and you were always so patient with my various foibles. Above all we had a lot of fun and were able to laugh together at all the many vicissitudes which made life much more bearable than it otherwise would have been. I don't know how things are going to work out here but I have my doubts as to their success. Anyway there are bound to be changes which as a founding member I probably won't appreciate. Well Johnny, I can't tell you how sorry I am that you have gone but I hope you will thoroughly enjoy your new job...'

An officer of the 3rd Battalion Welsh Guards wrote:

'I saw with great regret in Regt. Orders that you are leaving the Bde. It is very sad indeed but I don't doubt that you have had about enough.....I thought I would just write and wish you all good fortune in your new job and say how sorry I am that you have left us and also how grateful I have been for your tolerance and kindness in dealing with, I fear, a too often tiresome and querulous adjutant!'

Two officers of the 6th Coldstream wrote:

'I don't know how we will get on without you. I am sure your place will be difficult to fill and it will be some time before someone is found who can compete with your efficiency and patience, being an ordinary duty soldier I don't know how you do it.

and:

'I'm most upset to hear you're leaving us – selfishly that is for I guess it's a hell of a good job you're going to and you have just about earned a change of air. I shall miss you a hell of a lot and so will everyone else in the Bde. However good your successor may be, we shall never find anyone so tolerant and so human. I know quite well you must have stopped hundreds of rockets meant for Bns. and never passed on or only in the gentlest terms. As you know I knew nothing at all when we formed and goodness knows where I should have been without you and Col Bunty, bless him! Truly, Johnny, I'm enormously grateful for all your kindnesses, tolerance and forbearance – not to mention your jokes. If only a few more regular soldiers had your qualities, we shouldn't be in the general bog we are in.' (Rupert Hart Davis)

His time at 33rd Guards Brigade whilst not always a happy experience had not only deepened his skills in staff work but had also placed him at the centre of all matters pertaining to the Household Division and enabled him to get to know a wide variety of its leaders, many of whom he would meet again on the battlefield.

xcellent journey, marvellous place,
'e Fasses"
neymoon, Portofino (June 1937).

Christening of Serena Mary.
Born 24th May 1938.

Who is the smartest of them all? Front row, third from left. Company Commander, Training Battalion, Welsh Guards Colchester – January 1940.

The Welsh Guards

Outside West Newton Church, College Valley, Nr. Wooler, Northumberland. May 1941.

Company Commander, First Battalion, Welsh Guards, Elstree. (1940)

With Serena and Ginny,
May 1942.

GSO2 (Ops) HQ 8 Corps,
Taunton, August 1942.

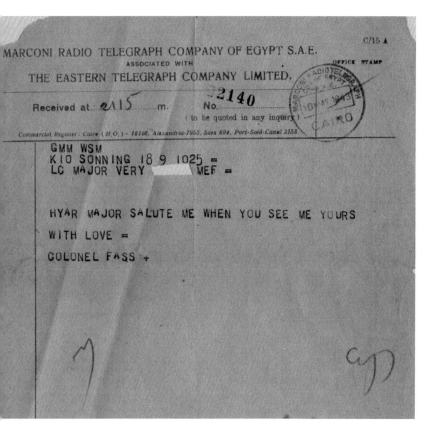

'…YAR MAJOR SALUTE ME WHEN YOU SEE ME
…URS WITH LOVE – COLONEL FASS' (May 1943).

Lieut.- Colonel GSO1 (Operations and Intelligence Liaison)
COSSAC, Norfolk House, St James' Square
March 1943 – January 1944

32nd Guards Brigade (1st Welsh Guards, 3rd Irish Guards & 5th Coldstream Guards) 29th/30th June 1944 in and around Cheux, facing 1 and 12 SS Panzer Divisions.

My Mother with the 'Baba' September
1944. Photograph by *Horrie* Noble

ck row from L to R: fourth, Aunt Joan Verey; fifth, Barbara Llewellyn (Godmother);
th, Sir Ernest Fass; seventh, my mother (wearing Welsh Guards brooch) and Michael
hn; eighth, Philip Verey; ninth, Robby Lawrence (Godmother); tenth, Lucy Verey;
venth, Godmother *Wizzel;* twelfth, Lady Fass; thirteenth & fourteenth, Nicholas Verey
arms) & Henry Verey.

ont row from L to R: first and second, Jill & Ann Llewellyn; fourth, Ginny; fifth, Serena;
th, Philippa Verey.

'To The Glory of God and in Loving Memory of John Fass, Welsh Guards who was killed in Normandy on 30th June 1944 when in command of the First Battalion aged 33.'
(St Michael's Church, Inkpen, Berkshire).

On leaving 33rd Guards Brigade he received the following marked War Office Urgent Memorandum which must have been a great relief from his troubles:

```
Acting Major J.E. Fass, Welsh Guards, Brigade Major, 33
Ind. Inf. Brigade (guards) is selected for appointment
as GSO2 (Ops) HQ, 8 Corps District with effect from 14
August, 1942, vice T/Major TRD Batt, Coldstream Guards,
to regimental duty.
```

Jefferson had written on it in pencil:

```
Fass will go down to Taunton Friday AM. Find out a train
and let 8 Corps know his time of arrival.  JJ.
```

8th Corps

In August 1942 after eight months with 33rd Guards Brigade my father was appointed as GSO2 (General Staff Officer Grade 2) with 8th Corps. Headquarters were in York but its formations were widely scattered and he joined one of its District HQs at Taunton in the West Country. He must have made a good impression on his senior officers in his earlier appointment as Brigade Major at 225th Brigade in Northumberland. The C-in-C was still Eastwood; Grasett, who was Canadian born, was the GOC 8th Corps and Money was still the Divisional commander of 15th Division of which 225th had been a part. Jock Whitefoord was Grasett's BGS (Brigadier General Staff). This job was in a higher formation and the Corps staff work was more advanced than that of a Brigade Major.

In September 1942, after a short leave salmon fishing together at Loch Fyne in Scotland, my father wrote to Horrie Noble as follows:

'I am now weaned from all other types of fishing except salmon and one day when we are both very old I will send you a photograph of Fass with his 60 odd pounder gaff, waders and all!. I miss you all very much. I have one telephone call which is fun from a local BM (Brigade Major) who I have known for some time but otherwise we are all very much on a "surname" standard and "Fass" is such an ugly name and never intelligible over a telephone. Still I like this job – the relief to be quit of JJ and no longer to be scared stiff when the bell rings is almost unbelievable.. people here know the last place was beginning to get me down. The GOC is first class, and the others are really very nice. It's a good job and an interesting one the pity of it is that none of us know whether we shall be disbanded or go on to bigger and better things as a Corps. I hope the latter. '

Horrie Noble wrote to me many years later of their time together in the West Country:

'We had such fun at Loch Fyne. I remember Johnny and I got up @ sparrowfart in order to fish but when Liza wanted to do something else one day your father immediately acquiesced and willingly tho' I know darn well that he was dying to have another go at the river. We had a never to be forgotten drive back from Somerset after an exercise and Johnny and I were thrilled with the glorious countryside. He and I were very much *en rapport* as you know. He was such a nice chap in everything.'

The highlight of his time at 8th Corps was the second of two great exercises held in Great Britain during WW2. The first was Exercise Bumper held in 1941 which practised repelling an invasion of Britain and the second was Spartan held in early March 1943 some six months after he had joined the formation that practised breaking out from a bridgehead in Europe. Co-incidentally, this scenario was one of the three alternative plans for Operation *Overlord* on which my father subsequently worked at COSSAC. My father was in Operations working for the BGS Jock Whitefoord who was responsible for 8th Corps planning, implementation and control. The exercise covered the whole of the South of England from Taunton in the West to Ipswich in the East and involved five Cops and ten Divisions. Manoeuvres took place over a three week period including an attack across the Thames on the line Reading-Oxford-Wallingford. Some of the main attacking forces involved were Canadian troops as well as a number of British armoured formations. The Times newspaper reported that Spartan was 'the greatest offensive exercise ever staged in the history of these islands' but afterwards the Canadian general in charge was dismissed and both Sir Bernard Paget of Home Forces responsible for training and Alanbrook the CIGS were critical of its results.

At the same time as my father was working furiously on the plans for Exercise Spartan at 8th Corps my mother was desperate to find a house where they could settle permanently rather than living in rented lodgings or staying at Bridge House with her parents. In the spring of 1943, and with the generous help of my mother's father, they were able to purchase Pound Cottage, Sonning, where my mother was excited at the prospect of being able to make a permanent home for them and their two girls, Serena and Ginny. She wrote of a time after the war had ended when they would 'enjoy each other from morning to night.'

There is a hint in my mother's correspondence that my father's performance in the exercise was being closely watched by his superiors and that his next appointment would depend on it when she wrote:

> '"Spartan" seems to be alright though it doesn't sound a wow somehow – I do hope you really have done well though if your position is so much a bottlewasher I don't see how you can make your name much either way.'

His superiors, however, must have been more than satisfied because his next posting took him to the very centre of the Allied war effort in the West.

Chapter Nine
COSSAC & D-Day Planner

'Plans are nothing but planning is everything'
(General Dwight Eisenhower, Supreme Allied Commander, Allied
Expeditionary Force)

Introduction

In May 1943 after seven months at 8th Corps and at the conclusion
of Exercise "Spartan" my father was promoted from Major to Lieut.-
Colonel. and appointed GSOI (Operations and Intelligence Liaison) at
COSSAC. It was then that his brother -in -law Michael Verey telegraphed
him from North Africa congratulating him on his elevation to the Staff
to which my father had replied *"Salute me when you see me".*

When both Grasett and Jock Whitefoord transferred from 8th Corps to
the new organisation, they took my father with them. They must have
gained a good impression of his competence as they had observed his
staff work and, in particular, his ability to get on with other people.
Grasett was appointed Head of Foreign Delegations in which post he
used my father on the intelligence liaison part of his duties and Jock
was the first Head of Intelligence for whom my father worked on
both operations and intelligence liaison matters. The formation of the
COSSAC organisation (Chief of Staff Supreme Allied Command) was
the result of the conference held in Halifax, Nova Scotia in December
1942 between US President Franklin Roosevelt and Great Britain's
Prime Minister, Winston Churchill. The decision taken then, which
was to plan for the re-taking of occupied Europe, was confirmed the
following year at the Quadrant conference in Quebec in August 1943.
The invasion would take place in mid-1944.

Operation *Overlord* was the Allies' greatest operation of World War II and the finest hour of Anglo-American co-operation:

'Only the British Empire and the United States could have successfully undertaken the largest and most dangerous amphibious assault in history. The operation was so complicated that the US Chief of Staff, General George C Marshall said of the plan 'it almost defies description'. The Allies assembled 2 million troops of numerous nationalities, nearly 5000 ships and 11,000 aircraft without the Germans knowing where or when the invasion would take place.' (Tucker)

This memoire is not the place to tell the full story of the D-Day plan, "Operation *Overlord*", or of the subsequent landings that began the battle for France on the 6th June 1944 and the liberation of Europe that followed. Suffice to say that much has been written about the actual event and the dramatic time that was experienced by all of those who were involved. The invasion was a supreme effort and it is widely believed that its planning and execution has never been surpassed in human experience for its originality, complexity and thoroughness. It was a triumph of the combination of strategic thinking and operational planning.

The landings involved not only the three British armed services: the Army, Navy and the RAF but also the strength of the United States military and a variety of other allied forces including those of France and Poland.

My father played an extraordinary role at the highest level of strategic command during the creation of the plan for "*Overlord*" in London and then fought in the front line in Normandy after the D-Day invasion had taken place. There were very few British officers of my father's age and rank who shared this unique experience.

In a letter that my father received after he had sailed for France, Robby Dundas wrote of a ditty that was circulating around Norfolk House:

*"Honour the brave, but see some praise remains
for such a large expenditure of brains".*

Setting the scene

However, in order to understand the background to my father's work, it is worth describing very briefly the overall situation of the Allies in 1943 and the immense difficulties and problems faced by its invasion planning staff at COSSAC. These problems included:

The strategic situation: By 1943 the British Army had been fighting for over three years throughout the world and between 1939 and 1942 had suffered a series of humiliating defeats including in France, Norway, Greece, Crete and Singapore. In the Western desert its single, and very recent victory, had been at El Alamein in November 1942. At Dieppe in August 1942, and in the first example in the second war of a seaborne attack on a defended coastline, a Canadian Division had been completely destroyed. British military leaders were therefore much concerned with the major losses and defeats that they had already suffered and were extremely doubtful of the potential for success given the obvious risks of an invasion over open beaches across the English Channel. They were all men who had experienced at first hand the slaughter of the First World War and they were continuously anxious throughout the planning process at the immensity of the undertaking and the very real prospect of its failure.

The three Allied leaders (Roosevelt, Churchill and Stalin) had met on a number of occasions to assess the progress of the war and to make plans for future victory. Throughout this time the Russians felt that they had been taking the brunt of the fighting against the enemy and had already suffered enormous casualties (for example their victory at Stalingrad in early 1943 had cost over 260,000 casualties). Stalin continually spoke of the need for a "second front" in Western Europe to take the pressure off his armies in the East and was disparaging about Great Britain's forces many of whom, he maintained, had not left its shores since the beginning of the war in 1939.

Churchill, his War Cabinet and the British Chiefs of Staff continued to hope that it would be possible to defeat Hitler and the Axis powers by attacking the so-called 'soft underbelly' of Europe which Churchill called his 'Mediterranean strategy'. They continued to pursue this approach after the defeat of Rommel in North Africa; the invasion of Italy via Sicily and on the Italian mainland after the Anzio landings. Churchill also had a particular fondness for operations in the Dodecanese and in Yugoslavia to achieve his aims whereas the Americans favoured a more direct attack on the European mainland, perhaps on the South of France. The Allies had already taken the risk of frittering away their scarce resources in the West in this way and by 1943 were experiencing an agonisingly slow and costly advance up the spine of Italy with much loss of men and materiel.

US forces were increasingly involved in the war against Japan to recapture their lost territories in the Philippines and to destroy Japan's army in the Far East. Whilst they had been willing to use Great Britain as a vast aircraft carrier from which their bombers could attack targets in occupied Europe as their contribution to the war in the West (by 1943 there were over 215 USAAF bomber units stationed in England), their main pre-occupation was in the Pacific. The American focus on the war in the Far East would become a major stumbling block faced by the *Overlord* planners. American plans for that theatre increased their need for landing craft to attack the Pacific islands and this became the paramount consideration for their ground and naval forces. There were simply insufficient of these vital craft to meet all of the strategic needs that had been identified by the Allied leadership for global operations that now included an attack on mainland Europe.

As a result, the initial plan for *Overlord* would involve no more than three Divisions of c. 45,000 men on a 30 mile front. This was to cause controversy when General B. Montgomery was appointed as the invasion force commander in January 1944. He immediately argued for a landing force of five divisions, two British, one Canadian and two US of 75,000 men. In the event, by the evening of D-Day on the 6th June 1944, c. 100,000 men had been landed.

Military politics: One issue the COSSAC staff faced initially was that of being taken seriously. There was much going on militarily at the beginning of 1943 with many calls on the attention of the British and

American Chiefs of Staff in the Middle and Far East. The problem for COSSAC was that it did not "belong" to the British Chiefs alone but was an equal and joint effort with the Americans. The organisation was the result of discussions between Roosevelt and his US Chiefs and Churchill and his British Chiefs but it was owned by neither and ways would need to be found to exercise its own muscle to get things done. Initially the RAF were particularly unhelpful as they thought that any plans would be a distraction from their main task of bombing Germany into submission. The RAF initially placed obstacles in the way of becoming involved or of making resources available for either reconnaissance or for the bombing of key targets such as railroads and beach emplacements. After early doubts the Royal Navy became enthusiastic supporters in their role of which was to carry the invasion force across the Channel and land it successfully on the shores of France.

Because of the partnership between the US and Britain at the highest level, the planning of the operation would be carried out by a joint planning staff composed of equal numbers of US and British staff. Staffs would have to work collaboratively and as a token of this on the first day of its formal activity at the beginning of April 1943, General Sir Frederick *Monkey* Morgan, its newly-appointed commander, summoned them into the canteen on the top floor of Norfolk House (in peacetime, a Lloyds Bank headquarters) in St James Square in London's West End and instructed each British officer to exchange one regimental cuff button with his opposite number on the US staff as a sign of their joint enterprise.

Morgan was an exceptional officer and military planner, a trusted friend of Alanbrooke the British Chief of Staff and from the same Corps, the Royal Artillery. Brooke told Morgan:

'Well, there it is. It won't work but you must bloody well make it!' The British and American military knew little of each other's ways and methods, but Morgan, a shrewd judge of talent, stitched his team together into an effective planning unit operating mainly from London and preparing for the biggest military operation in history – the Normandy invasion.' (Nicholas)

It was this Staff of seventy British and seventy US officers who carried out the basic planning needed to get more than a million men across the Channel with all their equipment with the first men planned to cross over and land on the French coast on D-Day, not later than nine months later by the 30th June 1944. As the *Overlord* plan developed an increasing number of military organisations from multiple services became involved and by the beginning of 1944 many thousands were employed in different locations. In January 1944 COSSAC was transformed into SHAEF (Supreme Headquarters Allied Expeditionary Force) on the appointment of General Dwight Eisenhower as its supreme commander.

The invasion planning staff & the issues they faced: The staff faced immense issues that were a series of questions to which they would need answers the first of which was where the landings should be made. The options stretched along the whole length of the Atlantic coast from Norway in the far North to Brest on the Western Atlantic seaboard. There were advantages and disadvantages to each location and hundreds of miles of coastline would need to be surveyed and assessed before a decision could be made. A landing somewhere on the French coast was considered to be the most likely destination

At the very beginning of the planning process advertisements were placed in the national newspapers appealing for pre-war holiday snaps of any part of the coast of France and from these a wall map was produced of its whole length on which suitable areas for invasion could be identified. The shortest route was between Dover and the Pas de Calais a distance of only 22 miles, but it was also the route that the Germans expected the Allies to take and it was heavily defended with steep beaches and cliffs that would be hard to enter.

The need to deceive the Germans into thinking that the landings would take place in the Pas de Calais became the focus for detailed deception planning and this activity would result in Hitler holding back a substantial proportion of his forces for an attack that he expected would take place in northern France. This meant that the German forces in Normandy where the actual landings would take place, were reduced - at least initially. The Western coast of France in Normandy was a much longer sea journey than to Calais but was less heavily defended and had the advantage of open beaches and a sloping shore. After much discussion it was decided that it would be to Normandy that the Allied armies would go.

The idea of landing all of the equipment that would be needed for a million men including vehicles, ammunition, fuel and all the other general stores across open beaches was a major concern and the planners had to find a port for this purpose that they could capture and use as quickly as possible after D-Day. Cherbourg was the obvious choice as it was in the same area as the Normandy beaches but it was used by the Germans as a naval base and was heavily defended. Someone had the brilliant idea of taking a temporary port with them on the invasion and anchoring it just off the landing beaches. It was code-named "Mulberry" and its construction of block ships and floating pontoons was to be towed across to Normandy to create a harbour and sheltered anchorage of 1400 acres. In the event. the "Mulberry" harbour was in place just four days after the invasion took place.

Another logistical question was how the thousands of vehicles that would be required for the battles ahead would be re- supplied with fuel. This was solved by the invention of a flexible pipeline that stretched under the sea from the English coast at Portsmouth onto the beaches the other side in Normandy. It was called "Pluto" and starting pumping fuel eight days after the invasion. Both "Mulberry" and "Pluto" were almost superhuman in their conception and application and were each an example of COSSAC's extraordinary creative planning effort.

Whilst the Germans did not know the precise point at which an attack would take place, they knew that it was coming and had fortified the coastline of Normandy with gun emplacements and beach obstacles that would at best frustrate and at worst prevent any landing from the sea. The planners had to first identify and then find ways to eliminate such obstructions so that landing craft and tanks would be able to get up the beaches. Continual reconnaissance was carried out by Royal Marines and Royal Engineers special forces who were landed by submarine to survey the beaches and assess their suitability for the landings. Special mine clearing devices and track-laying vehicles were designed to clear the obstacles on the beaches that would become known as "Hobart's funnies" named after the General in charge of their development.

Understanding the opposition that any Allied invading force could expect to face was a key activity for the *Overlord* planners and this was known as the enemy's "Order of Battle". Since the beginning of the War, the British had been listening to German signals and had developed all kinds of ways to penetrate them, the most famous of which was the work done at Bletchley Park in Buckinghamshire. Here Enigma code machines, stolen by Polish Intelligence officers from the German embassy in Warsaw before the war, and brought over to England, were used to decode enemy signals. My father would serve with the First Polish Corps in Scotland in early 1944.

Enemy signals arrived for de-coding at Bletchley from the Royal Signals *Y Service* (for Wireless Interception), a series of radio stations positioned up and down the East Coast of England that intercepted and recorded German signals. These messages would then be de-coded at Bletchley – that is when the code breakers could break the code – and turned into messages *en clair* that were known as "Ultra". Ultra would play a vital part in building up a picture of the opposing forces and their positions, strength and quality. This activity would have been a part of my father's duties on the staff known as "Operations A". Whether he was indoctrinated into "Enigma" and "Ultra" and knew what went on at Bletchley Park is not known but my mother told of him speaking about the origin of the intelligence that he received and used as coming from the "Y Service" so he should have known something about its provenance.

As planning advanced, other ways to identify the German Order of battle were used. These included aerial photographs taken by low flying fighter aircraft of the RAF's photographic squadrons and, nearer to the intended date of the invasion, reports from French agents of the Resistance on the ground in France who had instructions to send back intelligence about gun emplacements on or near the beaches where the landings would take place; roads and bridges; the location of German troops; unit badges and insignia and all railway movements of men and materiel.

Three COSSAC plans

During his time on the COSSAC staff my father worked on three different sets of plans that represented three alternative scenarios that had been provided by the Allied Chiefs of Staff and their Joint Planners. The D-Day planners were not working from a blank sheet of paper because since the beginning of the war Staff papers had been prepared by a number of different headquarters that had speculated about landings on the European mainland at some future date. The COSSAC staff were therefore 'heirs to a considerable fortune' and there was 'little needed of original work' what was needed by the COSSAC staff was 'cohesion and impetus' (Morgan).

The first of the three operational plans was named "Starkey" and was designed to force a lodgement onto the Continent in 1943 by breaking in somewhere on the coast of France which could then be held indefinitely. In this way German troops would be pinned down in the west and could not be used on the Eastern Front which would provide some relief for Soviet forces. Instead of an actual landing, "Starkey" became a major deception ruse as the British Chiefs of Staff could not imagine being ready in time to launch an attack onto the Continent in 1943. The "Starkey" plan, in which my father would play a part, became the source of a major controversy within the secret services (see below at 'The Secret War'). The second was named "Rankin" and was designed for use in the event of a sudden and unexpected collapse of the Nazi regime. This could occur, for example, if Hitler was assassinated and his leadership decapitated. This almost happened in July 1944 when an unsuccessful plot against Hitler was organised and a bomb was set off at his headquarters. Words such as the "wilting" of the enemy and "the rot setting in" were used to describe this scenario. The third plan, which was the one actually adopted, was named "*Overlord*" and planned for a full scale assault on mainland Europe using maximum force.

Each of these plans incorporated the lessons learned from their previous iterations to reach the time when "*Overlord*" was adopted as the final aim. In effect, the three plans were each a facet of the same plan. "Starkey", the first of the three plans, envisaged a diversionary attack on the Pas de Calais; "Rankin" a lodgement on the Cotentin peninsular and "*Overlord*" an attack on Normandy. The first plan was designed particularly to solve issues of flexibility in embarkation and landing and this required as much gathering of intelligence as possible. As a result the activity of the French Resistance was greatly increased and when the plan was terminated, there was much disappointment amongst them. However, "Starkey" had laid the foundations for the *Overlord* deception plan for the Pas de Calais region later named "Operation Fortitude" on which my godmother Robby Lawrence worked at "Operations B" that included MI5's (Military Intelligence) 'turning' of enemy agents.

Fortitude was the brainchild of the COSSAC staff that involved extraordinary efforts to deceive the Germans about the date and place of the invasion. The Staff created an entire non-existent US army stationed in East Anglia to mislead the enemy into believing that Normandy would be a feint and that the main invasion would be in the Pas de Calais. The ruse that included dummy landing craft in east coast ports, tanks made out of rubber and fake army signals reinforced German thinking that any invasion would come from that part of the English coast closest to France. In addition, *Fortitude* deceived the Germans into thinking that the Allies also intended to invade Norway. Both deception plans were completely successful.

At the end of the war my godmother, Robby Lawrence travelled to Germany as a member of a team to find out if the work of Operations B and MI5's *Doublecross* deception activities had made a difference to German decisions about troop deployments in the event of invasion. The team visited General Jodl, who had signed the surrender of the German army in May 1945 and who was imprisoned at Nuremburg for war crimes where Robby's father, Judge Lawrence, later Lord Oaksey, was President of the War Crimes Tribunal. Jodl was asked if Hitler had seen the final deception intelligence that had been designed to deceive him that the invasion would take place in the Pas de Calais and Jodl confirmed that this was most likely. As a result, key German formations were held back from Normandy in the initial stages of the battle that greatly helped the allied invasion effort. However, these formations would not be held back for long and when Hitler was persuaded by mid-June that Normandy did represent the main attack, the arrival of fresh Panzer divisions in Normandy was to play the major part in my father's death.

Operations "A"
The final plan for *Overlord* had to be in the hands of the Chiefs of Staff

by August 1943 and the pace of the work between April and August was relentless.

The role of the "Operations A" team, to which my father belonged, was to create an operational plan that would move a million men with all their fighting and logistical equipment from their bases in England first to the South Coast ports of embarkation, then across the Channel to the beaches of Normandy and finally into positions from which they could attack and defeat the German forces. It was a massive undertaking. Liaison required my father to work alongside of, and to integrate with, a wide variety of other organisations that were also involved in the planning process in addition to the COSSAC staff itself.. These organisations included other British Army (assault and attack formations), Royal Navy (beach reconnaissance and warship targeting of enemy land batteries) and RAF headquarters (aerial photography and bombing raids); attack formations including: special, airborne landing and Commando forces and liaison with other Allied and international forces, for example, the Canadian, Dutch, French and Polish armies stationed in Britain.

De Gaulle's Free French forces were going to be closely involved in the landings and the French also had an increasingly important part to play in intelligence gathering activities as the plans for *Overlord* were developed. Evidence of my father's liaison role was his friendship with De Gaulle's principal liaison officer to the British Chiefs of Staff. General Maurice Mathenet, who had attended the British Staff College in the 1920s. Mathenet had commanded in North Africa with Giraud and had to make his peace with De Gaulle before being appointed his Chief of Staff. He became a family friend and was intensely proud of what he described to my mother as "Mes belles Goumiers", his Moroccan troops who had a formidable fighting reputation.

In addition, the COSSAC planners needed to stay close to the planning and intelligence organs of the War Cabinet organisation. For example, COSSAC worked with the Joint Planning Staff responsible for advice to the British Chiefs of Staff and through them to the Cabinet and Prime Minister, to SOE (the Special Operations Executive) and MI6 (Military Intelligence abroad) who were responsible for running agent networks across the Channel. These were described as: 'all sorts and conditions of agencies in London' (Morgan) who were watching the enemy by land, sea and air. Liaison with US planners and US Chiefs of Staff in Washington was also required.

The Secret War

One consequence of his planning and liaison role at COSSAC was that my father became involved in the secret war of which there were a number that included SOE's activities in France whose role was to raise resistance and MI6's sabotage operations in addition to the organisation of radio deceptions and the running of double agents.

Operation "Starkey" was planned to take place in September 1943; was designed to test a number of aspects of the developing invasion plans and was to be as realistic as possible. It was directed towards the Pas de Calais in Northern France. Calais was the nearest point to the English coast and was the location from which the Germans might expect any invasion would come. One aim of the "Starkey" plan was to observe the way that the enemy would react to what became a major exercise that included practicing the logistics, communications and deception that would be needed for the real attack in 1944. The exercise was placed under the command of the RAF as it included the intensive aerial bombing of the Pas de Calais and the actual embarkation of troops from south coast ports protected by covering RAF fighters.

The plan also called for the involvement of SOE's agent networks in the area and this became something of an issue. By 1943 SOE's networks in France had become a significant potential source of support through their ability both to provide up to date intelligence about enemy formations and movements and to disrupt road and rail communications that would delay reinforcements towards the Pas de Calais, site of the supposed invasion.

However, at the same time the Chiefs of Staff were aware that a number of SOE's networks in France had been penetrated by German Counter-Intelligence and had become a risk to Allied security. The largest of these networks was code-named "Prosper" whose air landings controller, a Frenchman by the name of Dericourt, was believed to be a German spy

136

and responsible for the capture, torture and death of a number of SOE agents.

The Germans had to be made to believe that Operation "Starkey" was the real thing and not just an exercise and the Resistance fighters in France had to think the same. They were therefore instructed to move onto an invasion footing and to greatly increase their disruptive activities. Excitement in Northern France became intense and many acts of sabotage took place in response to instructions from London, some of which the Germans were aware of through Dericourt's treachery so that there were also many arrests.

In the event, the final secret signal for a general rising to be broadcast by the BBC was not received in France and subsequently it was understood that "Starkey" had been an exercise all along. The COSSAC staff had already warned that this would have a very bad effect on the morale of the Resistance and my father in his role in Intelligence Liaison with the French wrote COSSAC's assessment of its potential usefulness:

'Public opinion in all countries probably expects an attempt to be made this summer to open a *second front* by the invasion of France. No account has been taken in the plan for the repercussions this operation may have on public opinion, The repercussions in France might be such that patriots would no longer be prepared to play a part in a future invasion operation.'
(*Most Secret,* COSSAC/18DX/INT, an examination of the effects of Operation Starkey on Germany and the occupied countries, Lt. Col. JE Fass).

This memorandum makes it more likely that my father was indoctrinated into "Enigma" and "Ultra", as one part of "Starkey" had been to gauge German reactions to the operation and this would have been done by the interpretation of the enemy's signals that would detect any sudden changes in the deployment of their forces.

General Morgan's overall view about "Starkey" was:

We now know, from the best possible source, of the enemy's utter conviction of our intention to strike him in 1944 by way of the Pas de Calais. So firmly did he believe this that for a period of weeks after the Normandy landings had taken place, he clung to his theory that these were but a preliminary to the main blow that was to come upon him further North. To the extent that he held his reserves in hand in the Low Countries to meet this threat he feared so much when their timely intervention in Normandy might well have saved the day for him. Much happened after the days of COSSAC to drive home to the enemy the point made by Operation "Starkey", but there can be no doubt at all that all those who suffered inconvenience and worse in the summer of 1943 did so in the best of causes – ultimate victory'

(Morgan)

It is therefore somewhat ironic that my father should have been killed at precisely the time when the Germans finally decided that the attack on Normandy was the main invasion and released those same reserves from Northern to Western France in order to throw the Allies back into the sea.

Fortress Europe

Another way to understand what my father was doing at Operations A and Intelligence Liaison is to examine a document marked "Secret" and dated 20th September 1943 (found in his possessions) immediately after the final Plans for *Overlord* had been presented to the Allied Chiefs of Staff. This specified the way that COSSAC would be integrated with SHAEF before the actual invasion took place and listed its duties. These included:

```
COSSAC to be responsible for all intelligence in regard
to the area of Western Europe.
COSSAC responsible for coordinating "Y" policy.
Para-military. There is a definite requirement for the
study of all para-military/ Intelligence in the Theatre.
Extra accommodation will be required for Naval, Air
Force and visiting officers from lower formations during
planning.
The GI (Grade I Staff Officer, my father's rank and role) would
```

have a total of 69 staff that included 19 Intelligence officers and 35 clerks. The organisation would be responsible, inter alia, for:

Mapping
-Topographical maps
-Naval liaison for above
-Railways, roads, motor transport and fuel
Defences
-Artillery
-Flak
-Air Liaison for above
-Infantry and engineering defences
-Rearward areas supply dumps
Intelligence
-Airfield sites
-Rivers and canals
-Inundations and beaches
-Roads and bridges
Industries
-Water supply
-Electricity
-Local resources
-Oil and petrol storage
Order of Battle and troop locations
-Holland — Somme
-Somme — St Malo
-Remainder of France
-Camps

Within the Order of Battle further information and planning was required about the German army:

-Dispositions
-Identifications
-Strengths
-Reserves
-Moves
-Morale

Fortress Europe bristled with all kinds of obstacles, fortifications and elaborate defences including half a million foreshore obstacles; over four million beach mines and an opposing German army of 25 coastal divisions, 16 infantry and parachute divisions and 7 reserve divisions. Penetrating these defences would be an almost super-human task.

The document also shows, first, that it was a hugely complex task on which my father was engaged and, second, one of extreme urgency if the plan for *Overlord* had to be completed in seven months between April and August 1943. It also shows the way in which operations and intelligence were inextricably linked. The pace of work was intense and my father worked at least six days a week whilst living in a flat close to Norfolk House.

My mother told a number of stories about this period. One was an incident that occurred soon after my father arrived at Norfolk House. Security was very tight and as a way to check up on the possible leaking of information, security staff dressed as Royal Signals dispatch riders used to go and sit in the canteen and "chat up" the secretaries as they had their break. One day my father's secretary was in the canteen and a handsome sergeant sat down beside her. After introducing himself he asked her who she worked for. She replied "Colonel Fass". "And what does he do?" asked the soldier. "He is in Intelligence:, she replied. The soldier finished the conversation and left the canteen. A few minutes later my father's telephone rang upstairs in his office and he was told that he would never see his secretary again!

That same day he went through a list of ATS (Auxiliary Transport Service) personnel cleared for secret administrative work and spotted one Robby Lawrence whose name rang a bell as coming from a good family - her father was a racing man and a judge! Robby joined my father's office and became a life-long friend of the family and my godmother. In an interview for the BBC during the making of a film about the deception plans Robby said:

'I went for an interview at Norfolk House and was interviewed by someone called Colonel Fass of the Welsh Guards who seemed to me as old as the hills – he was probably in his thirties, I expect! And it transpired I think that he knew all about me before because he told me that it was a very special job and that they needed someone who was totally responsible and reliable and that sort of thing. It was the Operational planning for the invasion. Operation *Overlord* was being planned and the General in charge of Ops A in charge of COSSAC was General Morgan, who was a lovely man. And my General was called Whitefoord. Jock Whitefoord, and Johnny Fass was his G1.'

Robby described my father at this time as being "pugnacious" and "not suffering fools gladly". After the war Robby married Hugh *Cocky* Dundas, a famous Battle of Britain fighter pilot who was Douglas Bader's wingman and I was a page at their wedding. Soon after my father had been killed in June 1944 my mother asked her down to Pound Cottage at Sonning to meet her new born son. Robby later joined the Operations B staff responsible for deception where she worked closely with MI5 and '*Tar*' Robertson's agent-turning operation also known as *Doublecross.*.

Another story my mother told was of my father being summoned at any time in the day or night as a member of the COSSAC team that presented the current state of the invasion plans to the British Chiefs of Staff and War Cabinet as they were developed. This often took place underground and at night because the Prime Minister, Winston Churchill, sometimes did not get out of bed until 3pm in the afternoon and worked all night in his offices built deep below No. 10, Downing Street.

In October 1943 in a letter to her brother Michael serving in the Middle East, my mother wrote:

'Johnny would normally be champing at the bit but isn't, because he has such a terribly interesting and amusing job with never a dull moment. He has a lovely flat in London shared with a charming fellow worker.'

The *Overlord* plan was adopted in August 1943 and between September and January 1944 even more intensive planning activity followed that was designed to fill in the details. As General Eisenhower subsequently remarked 'Plans are nothing but planning is everything!'.

From COSSAC to SHAEF

In January 1944 a major change took place in my father's fortunes and those of the original COSSAC planning staff.

There had been much debate between the British and Americans about the arrangements for the overall – or supreme – command of the invading forces. Initially, Churchill had pencilled in Alanbrooke's name and had even discussed the appointment with him but as the pace of the build-up of men and materiel in Britain increased, the scale of the operation became even larger and the reliance on American support more obvious, it became clear that the supreme commander would need to be an American. General Dwight D. Eisenhower was commanding American forces in the Mediterranean; had the confidence of General Marshall, the US Chief of Staff, and was appointed the Supreme Commander. General Bernard Montgomery of the British Army was appointed to command the Allied ground forces which would be carrying out the actual invasion.

It had never been intended that COSSAC should become a permanent organisation. It had been created at a time when there had still been considerable doubt about whether a crossing to continental Europe would be possible in 1944. Its magnificent work had made this a reality. As a result, COSSAC had always possessed a sense of the temporary and provisional. Temporary, because the ability of the British to bring the war to a successful conclusion was now in the past: the British were exhausted by four years of war; there was an increasing shortage of manpower available for the attack and the population was reluctant to accept further losses after the disasters of Dunkirk, Singapore, Tobruk and Anzio. Provisional, because no one quite knew if it would be possible to pull off such an operation across the English Channel and against a defended shore. Churchill, in particular, was haunted by the disaster of Gallipoli in the First World War in which he had played a principal part.

For these reasons it was inevitable that the invasion would become an increasingly American *show* and that it should be led by battle-hardened commanders. In January 1944, with four months remaining before the planned invasion, a new team arrived in Britain to take command. The work of COSSAC was complete and the organisation became SHAEF - the Supreme Headquarters Allied Expeditionary Force - with Morgan, completely familiar with the plan for *Overlord,* being appointed its Chief of Staff. General Bernard Montgomery, who had been successful in the North African desert was appointed to command 21st Army Group who would make the actual landings and be ready to fight whatever battles that would be fought subsequently.

Montgomery had a very mixed reputation and was either loathed or admired. Whilst he had proved himself at the Battle of Alamein in the desert, his personal reputation was that he was arrogant and dismissive of any individual who he had not personally appointed and trained, or of any ideas that were not his own:

'He (Montgomery) was unpopular both with the troops and with many of the officers of the 1st Army. They felt he had won the desert battles on the backs of Wavell and Auchinleck and had become a tiresome and vain martinet who knew nothing about the kind of war experienced in North Africa and now being practised in Italy. It is true that the casualties in the Sicilian campaign had been excessive and that he was not doing well in Italy, while at the same time making a desperate bid to be in charge of the Second Front'. (Forman)

He arrived in London on the 21st of January 1944 to review the invasion plan and to make his personal contribution to it. Whilst much has been made of Montgomery's rejection of the *Overlord* plan and his trashing of those who had created it, in reality very little was changed. All of the intelligence about the enemy forces with which my father had been involved was in place and continued to be developed. Montgomery was scathing about the plan – describing it as "perfectly useless" but as Britain's only successful general he was in a strong position to make the changes he wished. In addition as the American invasion forces continued to be built up in Britain and so it became easier to argue for more landing craft which would now be diverted from the Far East to Europe. The increase in landing craft enabled Montgomery to land five divisions in Normandy instead of three originally planned and this was the only significant change that he made – so much for useless!

In the tradition of the British Army, Montgomery brought his own Staff with him who – to their credit - had experience of war fighting and had served him well in the Middle East. As a result of their arrival the entire British element of the senior COSSAC staff was dismissed in an unpleasant way and only two officers were invited to stay on - one of whom was my father!

My mother used to tell the story of how this happened. When Montgomery arrived at Norfolk House he demanded a briefing from each of the departments. At each of these meetings, Montgomery continually interrupted the presentations in his usual arrogant way except for my father's. My father displayed the map of the landing grounds on the wall behind him. He had practised all the night before the presentation using a pointer behind his back that would show the main German positions in Normandy. When he made his presentation the following day he was able to face Montgomery throughout it. Even Monty was impressed!

However, my father owed his loyalty to Jock Whitefoord and his other colleagues, both British and American at COSSAC and declined to stay on at what would now become SHAEF. Jock Whitefoord was shabbily treated and was obliged to take a job as the Chief of Staff, West African Forces , which he greatly resented as it was far from the centre of the war effort. Montgomery had a group of his own trusted officers who would take over the Intelligence role.

At the end of January 1944 my father left the COSSAC/SHAEF Staff and Jock Whitefoord , COSSAC's first chief of Intelligence and his immediate superior, appraised his work:

```
Supreme Headquarters
Allied Expeditionary Force
G-2 (Intelligence) Division
28th January 1944

To: COS (chief of staff)
```

1.In view of the change in MG (Int) and Lt Col Fass's
lack of former intelligence experience, both Maj-Gen
Whiteley and I agree that it would be better if a new
head was appointed to the Operational Intelligence
Section, now that I am leaving.
2.Lt-Col Fass has done outstandingly good work while with
HQ SHAEF. His drive, energy and enthusiasm have been of
the greatest value in getting our machine working.
He has worked in very close and happy co-operation with
the Naval and Air Intelligence Sections. He has run a
very happy staff and has given me the most loyal support.

3. I have seen Lt-Col Fass work as the BM of an Infantry
Brigade, GSO 2 (Ops) of a Corps and now as G.1 (Int).
He is a very able, efficient and loyal operational staff
officer

I recommend that he should now be employed as a GSO 1
with a Division of the Field Force.

If no suitable operational appointment is now available
in the field force, I consider Lt-Col Fass should be
allowed to go back to a Field Force Battalion of his
regiment in order to give him a chance of getting
command.

P Whitefoord
Major General
A C of S
G-2 (Intelligence) Division

and, again from Jock:

An absolutely loyal officer, with very high qualities
of energy, drive and initiative. Very popular with his
subordinates and gets the best out of them. Very quick
and hard working. A first class operational staff officer
or potential commander.

Advancement on the Staff — Yes
GSO 1 of a Filed Force Division

```
After command as BGS of a Corps
Advancement in command of troops — Yes
2nd in command of an Inf Bn — with a view to getting
command

P G Whitefoord
Major General
Home Forces
28 Jan 1944
```

Major General Whitely, Jock's replacement as the new Assistant Chief of Staff, Intelligence at SHAEF who had been Montgomery's BGS Intelligence in North Africa, wrote to my father whilst he was on leave in February:

```
Room 124
Norfolk House
St James's Square
SW I

25th February 1944

Dear Johnnie,
Gannon has rung me up and ticked me off for not having
sent you to join the Poles before this. I told him that
you were on leave and that it would not be contemplated
that you should interfere with so important a matter.

He agreed quire readily that it would be time enough for
you to join the Poles on the expiry of your leave.  So
will you work to this.

This conversation of Gannon's was quickly followed by
General Grasett putting the heat on.  You are very
popular!

I have heard no more about Henry Foord, but have arranged
with Gannon that you can come down to hand over to him if
in the end he does arrive and thinks it necessary.
Should Henry Foord not turn up, I must make it clear to
```

you that I intend to do all that I possibly can to get
you back.

Meanwhile, I hope that you are enjoying your leave and
forgetting about the minor problems of War.

Yours ever,
John Whiteley.

(Gannon was Major-General in charge of Administration at COSSAC now
SHAEF; Major-General Grasett remained Head of Foreign Delegations;
Foord was my father's replacement as G1 Intelligence and Whiteley was
Jock's replacement as Major-General, Head of Intelligence).

This correspondence referred to two aspects of my father's remaining
career. The first was to the Poles. My father's next appointment was to
the Polish Army in exile stationed in Scotland where he would take up
the position of G1 and Senior Liaison Officer between SHAEF and the
Poles which would be closely related to the work that he had done at
COSSAC. His task would be to brief the Poles about the Operations and
Intelligence aspects of their role in the forthcoming invasion and the part
they would play in it. As Whiteley's letter implied, this meant that his
connection with *Overlord* was not completely ended as Grasett was still
responsible for Foreign Delegations at SHAEF and would have been
responsible for this appointment to an Allied formation.

The second reference was to the prospect of his return to the Field Force
and becoming second in command of a battalion with a view to getting
command – presumably in the invasion. This was an echo of the previous
correspondence with Dudley Ward and the Welsh Guards before he went
to the Staff College in January 1941. My mother wrote of this time to
her brother in a letter dated February 1944 about my father's situation:

'You are quite right about J – firing off some bullets is just what he is
now trying to do but not finding it easy. He is definitely leaving his
present absolutely super job that has been sheer heaven for us both
as well as do exactly what you say and his superiors and sponsors,
where he is now, were very keen for him to command one of his
Bns. But unfortunately there is no chance of it as there are only 3

147

and several people to come before Johnny's turn including even 2nd in Command so that's no good at the moment. He has just refused another job because it's in London but isn't sure if this refusal is going to be taken or what is going to happen so rather miserable. Anyway they all are – as since the new arrivals so many changes and no one knows where they are or what they'll be doing next - in consequence very low morale at the moment amongst all and sundry.'

The end of my father's time at COSSAC also marked the end of, what I believe, was the pinnacle of his professional career. During this time he had made a vital contribution to the planning for the Invasion; he had worked at the highest level of the politico-military effort of the war and had rubbed shoulders with some of the most senior and distinguished military figures of the time.

As the reports both remarked upon and implied, the British Army was a tribal organisation and Montgomery wanted his own people around him; my father had no direct war-fighting experience in Intelligence compared with the new team and he acknowledged his need for front-line experience before he could reach higher rank.

British Liaison HQ – The First Polish Corps
At the end of his leave at the beginning of March 1944, my father travelled North to a new job as G1 at No. 4 British Liaison HQ responsible for working with the Polish Army Corps stationed in Scotland. His office was at 44, Mortonhall Road. Soon after I had made a programme about my father for the BBC on the 50th anniversary of D-Day in 1994 called *Relative Losses,* I received a letter postmarked Falkirk which read:

'.......I am pretty sure that I served under your father in 1944. I was an NCO in the British Liaison HQ with the Polish Forces in Scotland and our CO was a Lt-Colonel Fass. He left us to rejoin his regiment some time before D-Day and we were saddened to hear that he was killed in Normandy'. (Brooks)

My mother reported that he was not happy in Scotland and this was partly due to the sad situation in which he found many of the Poles with whom he worked. They had been exiled from their homeland for over four years and many of them had received no news of their families throughout all of this time. It was also something of a backwater after COSSAC and my mother wrote:

'What a shame it is you aren't in a good job where you're happy, it does seem such rotten luck, but perhaps the luck will change and Jack G (Gannon) will really do something for you'.

and

'Your job sounds as bum as it can possibly be, it is sickening, but what with the changes in your Regt. and Monty coming and one thing and another you never know your luck. I think to bring George Browning back (newly appointed to command the 1st Battalion, Welsh Guards - author's note)) a thoroughly retrograde step and shows poor selection of possible and high time they got a move on to people like you.'

Typically, he found it difficult settling into his new job. He wrote to Robby Lawrence:

'16th March 1944

'One hates new places but I've seldom been so sick of heart as here.....My job is the end. There is an armoured and unarmoured side to the Mission. The armoured deal with Armd. Div. and live down at Drybrough Abbey a heavenly place on the Tweed. I as head of the un-armoured side have about 12 officers and 40 ORs (other ranks) and deal with all the static schools and whatnot. I spend my time here inspecting billets and cookhouses and having the place scrubbed out. There was no organisation, no orders, no nothing. Never mind, let's hope I won't be here for long. Monty came to inspect all the Poles on Monday and Grasett (who was already asking for my father's return to SHAEF) on Tuesday. It was great fun and he really did just what was required and quite charming. Boosted up morale no end and my opinion of him went up more

149

than I had meant. I too miss you all a great deal. Remember me to them <u>all</u>.'

In late March my mother wrote to him saying:

'You seem to be having a very nice time all the same, and to be with nice people, which is at least something. And though it's <u>damn</u> bad luck, I shouldn't feel any shame or disgrace, because I'm sure you weren't sent with that motive, it is pure bad luck and nothing else, I am sure and expect you will be surprised how quick you get a move – after all you already have 2 stakes, one in your Regt. And one through Monty and Kit Dawnay (Montgomery's personal assistant and lifelong West Downs school friend – author's note) and should think the reason you've had no reply from the W.G (Welsh Guards) is because the thing isn't settled and they don't know what exactly is going to happen which in a way means there is hope.'

It is clear that my father felt that the way that Monty and his men had swept in so arrogantly and treated the COSSAC Staff so badly was a personal slur on his good name and on the quality of the work that he and his colleagues had done at COSSAC. My mother wrote: 'How <u>awful </u>for Jock Whitefoord, he has been badly treated, hasn't he?' My father probably also felt that Scotland was not so much punishment but banishment from the centre of affairs.

By mid-April he had as always recovered his poise and wrote to his mother:

'14th April

If the 2nd Front was not starting in the near future this job might be quite fun – the people are congenial and Chris Peto the Commander of the Mission very nice – I live in the office billet here and have a barish room with a troops bed – a couple of tables and not really much else. My office is across the passage......I've a lovely green and very smart bathroom which makes it all bearable. I have a troops breakfast which is quite adequate and not bad especially when I manage to buy some eggs at one of the farms we pass when

motoring. I lunch and dine at the New Club – a very good one and the 'smart' place in Edinburgh – everyone is a Lord or Master of something generally 102 or rather doddery but the food is good and it makes all the difference. The other officers are very pleasant and I'm a sort of tin God and addressed as 'Sir' and rather grovelled to (they have not seen a real soldier before). I go round like Gen Monty inspecting various schools (weapons training, etc.) and all the usual sort of inane questions that all generals ask ie 'What part of Poland do you come from? Oh, really very interesting'. Never having heard of the place they say in my life. The Poles are <u>very</u> nice –rather pathetic and quite hopeless – very slav. I find it very tiring to have to concentrate on their broken English. I drive all over Scotland through the most lovely country. Generally down to the Tweed – to Kelso, Melrose – Peebles and so on but I've been up on a trip to Perth and on up to Taymouth. It's not a worthwhile job and soon I should leave and do some real soldiering. I'm quite busy and quite enjoying it but I feel far away.
Johnny'

My father's first cousin was Robert Morley, the actor and son of one of Sir Ernest's sisters who had married a Major Morley. Robert was acting in a play in Edinburgh with Beatrice Lillie, one of Britain's favourite actresses. Robert wrote about my father in his Memoirs *Responsible Gentleman:*

'I had a cousin who was killed in the war, young, very good-looking and lively. He had been seconded from his regiment and given a job on the general staff, and I met him in the month before "D" Day. It so happened that we were both in Edinburgh one evening, and he saw the show, and I asked him to have supper with me and Bea Lillie afterwards. Bea had lost her son some months before and perhaps in some ways John reminded her of him. They took an instant liking to one another, and we saw a good deal of him for a short while. He used to turn up casually and come out to supper and then go back to wherever we were staying, and amuse Bea. She was not an easy person to get to know but John understood her and took immense trouble to please her. It was rather a bleak tour, in a play which I had written and which resisted all our efforts to turn into a success, and

151

his visits were for Bea the one thing she looked forward to. Then suddenly, they ceased. He had rejoined his regiment about a week before "D" Day and was killed in Normandy a week later. I had asked him one evening whether he thought he would stay in his job until the end of the War. "No" he said, "I don't think I'd care to do that. Sometimes it's nice to be with the regiment" I knew exactly what he meant. The curious thing was that he was the one to be embarrassed'. (Morley & Stokes)

On his departure from Scotland General Dorata the Commander of the Polish Forces whose troops would soon follow my father into battle in Normandy, wrote:

April 19th 1944

Dear Colonel Fass,

I felt nothing but regret when I was told that you were leaving us to return to your regiment.
I would like you to know how much your co-operation and help you accorded us are appreciated and how pleased we all have been to have you with us.
On behalf of the officer of my Headquarters and in my own name I express to you best wishes for your future work and of your personal well-being.

Yours very sincerely,

Dorata

When my father went to say goodbye to the officers of the Polish Corps an event took place about which my mother used to speak with admiration. In a letter to his mother Winnie he wrote:

'I had a touching birthday rather as I went over to the Polish Corps who somehow had found out (that it was my birthday) and besides making me incredibly nice speeches saying how much and so on they would miss me they all drank my health and gave me a birthday cake with 33 candles and when they knew I had children insisted on my taking it away with me for them. Isn't it kind. The children will be thrilled. I feel quite sad at leaving this place in a way. I have enjoyed it and it has been a great change but one really could not sit here out of the Second Front not even having fired a shot in anger in this war. It will be fun to get back to the Regiment though an awful wrench to have to go and know that instead of being able to get down for weekends to Sonning I shall have to wait 6-8 months or so. I believe we shall see the end of the German war by the end of this year.'

When he left the Liaison job in Edinburgh he wrote to General Morgan now joint Chief of Staff at SHAEF (perhaps to remind Morgan of his existence!) and advised him of his next move. Morgan replied:

4th May 1944

My Dear Johnny,

It was very nice of you to write to me on the 3rd May and tell me of the latest change in your fortunes. Though I am sorry to hear that you have been obliged temporarily to relapse to so lowly a station, it is nevertheless good to have you writing so cheerfully. This move will at any rate get you back in the line that I know you were really keen on following. I hope it will not be long before you are commanding a battalion.

I am glad to see that in retrospect you got something out of your short stay with the Poles. As you say, they are charming but hopeless people. One cannot help but be saddened by thoughts of the prospect of what lies before these particular Poles who have been soldiering with us here. But I hope and trust that your estimate of the Russian situation is the right one and that the Poles are over-pessimistic. Personally I subscribe to your view.

The best of luck to you in what is to come and I hope as you do that we shall get together again, preferably on the far bank.
Yours ever,

F E Morgan

153

Both my father and Morgan were wrong about the Russians and their long term intentions which included the conquest and subjection of the whole of central and eastern Europe. The Polish Corps fought very bravely in Normandy from July 1944 onwards and in particular their armoured and infantry units helped to close the Falaise Gap where over 250,000 retreating German soldiers were taken prisoner and where the campaign in western France ended. At the end of the war many of the Corps returned to Poland in the expectation of freedom but in 1948 the Russians imposed the tyranny of communist rule and anyone who had fought with the British was not allowed to work. Some were able to leave Poland and came back to Scotland where a thriving Polish community remains to this day.

It would be 47 years later in 1991 that I set off on my first trip to Poland eighteen months after that country's liberation from over 40 years of communist rule to work for the British Government on economic reform. I carried in the pocket of my waistcoat an arm badge of the Polish Corps that my father had worn all those years earlier in Scotland.

After only three days leave at Pound Cottage, he was posted back to his Regiment to prepare for Operation *Overlord* and on 4th May 1944 was appointed as 2 Company Commander, 1st Battalion, Welsh Guards, a lorried infantry battalion in 32nd Guards Brigade, part of the Guards Armoured Division. He was back in the Field Force where he had started as a young man aged nineteen and had returned to the Brigade of Guards in which he was commissioned.

My mother wrote:

> 'I'm all for you doing the right thing and fighting, etc. but it seems hard it couldn't have been in a better capacity after where you've got to – and anyway I'm only worried in your survival. Nothing else. You can fight with 50 Bns. If you only aren't killed.'

and

> 'What shall I do when you are 2nd Fronting – so soon now – just when I'm at the end of my 9 months (the baby was due on the 15th

154

June) and shall want you so badly to see the baba, etc. but as long as you aren't actually killed, I can bear almost anything. Remember that you are everything to me and I shall be completely hopeless without you...,..because after 4 ½ years war we now have so little time.'

He had a little over eight weeks of his life remaining.

Chapter Ten
NORMANDY! AH, NORMANDY!

Operation *Overlord*

Inscribed on the walls of the memorial at the British war cemetery at Bayeux to all those who fell in Normandy are the words:

Nos A Gulielmo Victi Victoris Patriam Liberavemus
(We, once conquered by William, have now set free
the Conqueror's land.)

In the first week of June 1944 Field Marshall Erwin Rommel, Commander in Chief of German Forces in Western France, had decided to take a short break back in Germany with his family. Rommel was Germany's best known general who had made his name fighting in Italy in the First World War and had led the Afrika Corps in North Africa that had surprised and out-manoeuvred the British on many occasions until defeated at the battle of Alemein in October 1942.

Since his appointment to command in western France Rommel had driven up and down the coast inspecting and re-enforcing its defences against possible invasion. Rommel was an expert at military strategy and from his earliest assessment of where the Allies might land he had his suspicions - unlike others in the German High Command - that it would be in Normandy although recognising that this would be a daunting undertaking for the Allied armies.

When Rommel was first told of the initial landings in Normandy on the 6th June he is reported to have driven a clenched fist into the palm of his open hand and to have declared: "Normandy! Ah, Normandy! They would come to Normandy!"

However, it would another two weeks after D-Day before the Germans, and Hitler in particular, would accept that the landings were not a feint; it was still believed in Berlin that the main landings would take place later in the Pas de Calais. As a result a number of major German units were held back in Northern France and by the time that they were released - some of them arriving in Normandy just in time to fight in the battle in which my father was killed – it would be too late to throw the Allies back into the sea. COSSAC's *Fortitude* deception plan had worked superbly!

It had to be Normandy for a number of obvious reasons that the *Overlord* planners had calculated, including access to it from the south coast ports in Britain, and its open beaches. In addition, because of the success of the *Fortitude* deception, the defences in Normandy, although representing a formidable obstacle, were not as well developed as those in the North; nor were all of its troops of the first quality.

However, as well as making good military sense, there were other reasons for selecting Normandy as the point of attack. The relationship between England and Normandy had been close for almost 1000 years. It was from Normandy that Duke William the Conqueror had set out on his invasion in the autumn of 1066 and his successors, the Plantagenet kings of England, claimed also to be Dukes of Normandy. Throughout England's history there had been close ties between the adjoining kingdoms and when the British soldiers fought in Normandy they were amazed to find that not only was the countryside similar to the West Country from which many of them came but that the place names in the villages through which they marched or drove carried the same surnames as their own such as Granville (Grainville), Seymour (Saint Maur), Tracey (Tracy-sur-Mer) and even included the name of their commander Montgomery (Montgomerie)!

The *Overlord* plan called for the landing of five Divisions of British, Canadian and American troops in five designated beach locations along the coast east and west between Caen and the Cherbourg peninsular.

These troops would be assembled at ports along the South Coast between Gravesend in the Thames and Plymouth in the south-west and would be carried across the western English Channel in convoys of ships commanded and co-ordinated by the Royal Navy.

One difficulty that the planners could not have imagined was quite how rough the sea would become during the early days of June 1944, with the Channel experiencing its worst storms for over 100 years. As a result, the invasion was delayed by 24 hours which was already several days after the first troops had been loaded into their transports. The Supreme Commander, Eisenhower, came close to cancelling the whole expedition and wrote a letter to be published in the event of failure. However, D-Day 6th June would be a stunning success with over 100, 000 troops landed in the first 24 hours and a "lodgement" made on the French coast that the enemy would fail to remove.

When the troops had been successfully landed and had been re-inforced to over 1 million men, the Allies would advance into Normandy and spread out to attack key enemy targets and troop concentrations and destroy them. The immediate purpose was to capture the Port of Cherbourg on the western flank to provide a harbour for the unloading of stores and to capture Caen on the eastern flank, Normandy's capital city and centre of rail communications. Then, it was intended to break out of Normandy, cross the Loire, move towards Paris and liberate the rest of France. None of this could occur unless the landings could be sustained and the enemy could be brought to battle and decisively defeated in Normandy.

The strategy therefore required that the Germans should be provoked into attack and this was referred to by Montgomery, the Allied ground commander, as intentionally "sucking in the enemy". This would take place on the eastern flank around and beyond Caen. However, it turned out to be much more difficult country in which to advance and much easier for the Germans to defend than anticipated as the mainly untried British and Canadian troops pushed forward to make contact and to fight. My father was killed in the second of a series of such major Allied attacks.

The battle for Normandy took longer and was harder than had originally been planned. The mainly novice Allied armies on both flanks faced enemy troops who had been fighting since 1939, the best of whom had returned from the savage campaign on the Russian Front. They were battle-hardened and had much more experience of war fighting, particularly in all-arms co-operation, that is, infantry and armour (tanks) working together in battle groups that included guns and combat engineers.

An even more serious consequence of the enemy's long experience was that generally their equipment was superior and this applied, in particular, to their tanks and guns that were more powerfully armed. The Allies therefore faced the full might of an enemy that was well prepared, well led and well equipped. By the time of the break out at the end of August 1944, three months later, 56,000 Allied soldiers would be dead and the lovely Norman countryside would have been turned into a chaotic killing ground that equalled the ferocity of the battles of the Somme twenty eight years earlier in 1916.

Preparation & Assembly

The message sent by General Dwight Eisenhower, Supreme Commander Allied Expeditionary Force, to his forces on the eve of the Invasion read:

> *You are about to embark upon the great crusade toward which we have been striving these many months. The eyes of the world are upon you.......I have full confidence in your courage, devotion to duty and skill in battle.*

My father re-joined the First Battalion on 4th May 1944. By that date the Battalion had moved down from Yorkshire and was billeted in a holding camp outside of Eastbourne prior to embarkation. There was a sense of both anticipation and foreboding at what lay ahead and for my father the added concern of re-entry and re-adjustment into the world of "The Regiment" and the imminent arrival of his third child expected on the 14th June. A guardsman in the Battalion wrote:

> "I doubt if there is a man in the Battalion who, given the opportunity, would back out of the invasion now. For four years we have had it

easy here in England. I think we all feel we owe it to our own people, the munitions workers, the firemen, the bombed and homeless.... and above all to our own conscience, to do our stuff now. It "takes us" and we know it'.

(Murrell)

My father wrote to his mother Winnie:

'I wish this 2nd Front would start. We are all beginning to get sick of hanging about waiting'.

On the 4th May when he left Pound Cottage, Sonning to join the First Battalion he wrote to my mother:

'Don't worry about me. I will come back to you I swear and safe and sound. This is a sort of trial by fire that I have to go through. It's something I can't avoid and without doing so could never meet people again and be able to look them in the face. It's hell though just the same and sitting back on the Staff one forgets what hell it is really. Rather scruffy billets full of men – a bare room for a bedroom with nothing - Not being allowed to take any kit at all.. Most of what I have taken will have to come back I'm afraid. Hundreds of officers in a mess. Masses of soldiers continually saluting – oh ghastly BUT you know me in new places and there are a lot of friends.

George (Browning, Commanding Officer) not altered in any way. James Gresham another Company Commander – charming Cyril Heber Percy very nice and one or two others although I know none of the younger mess. I believe my Company to be only fair by all accounts and I have as 2nd in Command Eddie Beddinfeld not my first choice.

I have had a great welcome from some of the NCOs and men I used to know which has been rather nice – the drill Sgts and Sgt Majors and so on. But Oh God what a sort of out of the frying pan into the fire and what a change from Norfolk House and the Poles. Joe's Bn is just over the road so maybe I shall see him tomorrow. We get 24 hours leave every week so we must organise that.

All I want to say you know its that I love you and adore you and miss you dreadfully and as time goes on I shall miss you more. I do hope you are alright and that things will go well with you in everything.'

and later on the same day:

'My first day has passed fussing over the usual petty little things that Regimental officers have to fuss over – all completely trivial really but important if the thing is to go smoothly and well. I've a nice Sergeant Major though perhaps stupid and a v. nice Quartermaster Sergeant. The Company look better than I had thought I'm glad to say. I went round to see Joe today to find that he was away at brigade but I saw many from the old 33rd Bde days who gave me a great welcome.

The weekly leave from camp enabled my parents to meet either at Pound Cottage or in London over this period of waiting both for the invasion to start and for my birth.

'It was brilliant of you to come up to London as I feel that I had seen you for much longer than just 24 hours. The children were divine too weren't they. Serena looking like a vision and little Ginnie so pleased. Wonderful to have such a welcome and all the more damnable to be going 2nd Fronting just as they are growing up. Saw Gen Alan Adair (Major General commanding the Guards Armoured Division) this pm who was very pleased to see me and so nice.'

Eastbourne was close to where one of his former *lovelies*, known by him as Wizzel, lived with her husband Humphrey, a senior civil servant and their two children. My father visited them on a number of occasions whilst encamped at Eastbourne.

He also visited old friends at 8th Corps and reported:

'I had tea with 8 Corps – met a lot of old friends and saw Henry Floyd the BGS. Several of them sighed and said that they wished I was back as G1!

My father had not served in the Line for some considerable time and on occasion found it hard to re-adjust:

'I have now got a "Mr Philip" face (this was a reference to Philip Verey, his brother in law when he used to return from TA weekend exercises – author's note) bright red and rather unshaven because we've no electricity in our billet but at last hot water and I had my first bath for a week yesterday!. My feet were very sore after unwonted exercise the first for 3 1/2 years. What heaven it will be to see you again. This coming year is going to be such hell. We must never stay in the army a minute longer that is necessary so that we can be together and have a normal married life that we've missed for 5 years. These people are sort of hard to make friends of – its probably a matter of time. All the same I'm glad I'm back – one's in the swim and I'm looking forward to it really.'

and

'Nothing is worse than being by oneself in one's own particular misery and one desperately wants someone to talk to. I've been doing really very little except inspect this and that and fettle round. I go marching tomorrow so think of my poor feet – actually it ought to be quite fun. It's appalling to find in what a tiny world everyone lives in – bounded by the Bn and petty personalities and affairs - So different to Norfolk House days when one swung numbers about with such éclat with and of the mighty. Rather good for one I suppose. People are very nice to me but one feels strange and of course I know none of the junior officers at all. I quite enjoy it all but were I to stay for very long feel that one would become completely atrophied and hopeless.

On June 4th in response to an anxious letter from my mother my father wrote:

Don't please think that I will not come back to you it would be the most stinking luck and I could not bear it either....and pray that we may be together again soon and for always. I have to go through with this thing. It would have been so easy to continue to sit at SHAEF

163

safe and sound but both you and I know that it simply would not have done. So many others are in the same boat and I would not miss it for the world. This is a good battalion and if this thing goes really well there is no reason why the Germans not pack up just like they did in N. Africa. Pray for me from time to time and I shall be alright.'

However, he did not give up on his connection with the Staff and wrote the same day:

'I went to some sports they were having this afternoon and found lots of friends among both officers and men. Henry Floyd was v. nice and I talked to him for quite a long time.'

At the sports an incident occurred that he particularly remarked upon that was an echo of his earlier life in the pre-war army:

'Who should I see but the late RSM of the Berks who you remember was RSM at the Depot when I was Adjt. there. He is now a major!! And Camp Commandant at Corps HQ – quite insufferable in going out of his way to call officers by their Christian names although I'm glad to say he never called me Johnny and slipped up into a couple of involuntary 'sirs'.

At the end of May after less than a month back with the Battalion and after no more than two or three flying visits to his home or to London, the waiting was finally over and the Second Front began. On the 6th June, my father wrote:

'It has come at last. This big day and in it you see some of the hard work and long hours that I and Jimmy and Kenneth put in last year. When you think about it it's a wonderful time because if it goes as it should and I believe it will it's the start of the end of the war. I feel terribly out of it just now and can picture the tremendous activity and interest that is now the lot of Henry Floyd who is sitting in my chair but later on the tables will be reversed and whilst he may be able to see the big picture I shall be really in it – not miles away – and Robin (Rose Price) and Michael (Verey) and the rest of them will have had it from the point of view of saying I'm just a b. Staff officer. You are probably missy that it has all come just at this time and worried for us. My Company is shaking down and I'm getting to know and like then.'

The Landings

Inscribed on the colonnade at the American cemetery and memorial above Omaha beach in Normandy are the words:

This embattled shore portal of freedom is forever hallowed by the ideals, the valor and the sacrifice of our fellow countrymen.

2,700 vessels were steaming towards Normandy from ports along the south and south west coast and 195,000 sailors manned the invasion fleet, carrying 130,000 troops, 12,000 vehicles, 2,000 tanks and 10,000m tons of stores.

The initial landings took place at day-break with a force of over 50,000 men storming the beaches from landing craft and whilst there were some disasters – particularly on one of the American beaches, code-named Omaha - the main force was lodged successfully just inland from the Norman shore.

A historian later commented:

'The D-Day landings of 6 June represented the greatest feat of military organisation in history, a triumph of planning, logistics and above all human endeavour. The massed airborne assault on the flanks that began in darkness, the air and naval bombardment followed by the dawn dash up the fire-swept shoreline by more than 100,000 British, American and Canadian engineers, infantrymen, armoured crews and gunners, achieved brilliant success'. (Hastings)

The following day, as tensions rose about the day he would be crossing to France, my father wrote furiously to my mother on the 7th June:

'If you can't be more sensible and stop asking stupid questions as to when I am going over the telephone I shall not ring up again for there is 100% censorship. MADDENING of you.'

The baby was due on the 14th and on the 13th he wrote to his mother that he had been able to get home on the evening of the 12th. How he managed to break out of the very tight security cordon thrown right around the South Coast and how he acquired a motorbike, we shall never know:

'Wasn't it a bit of luck that I managed to get back for Sunday night to Pound Cottage. I had hoped that the baby might have arrived over this week-end. It was not due until the 14th tomorrow but had got ready to arrive and Lisa thought it might come last Thursday. Typically though it has made no move since. It was a pity because its hard to get away and I should have liked to have see the baba before I have to go. We had a heavenly day. We borrowed a pony and took Serena for a ride in the morning which she adored and then little Virginia rode in the afternoon and loved it too and was very good and sat up straight as a rod.

and he wrote to my mother on the same day:

'I spite of not being there to see the baby, in spite of the hell of saying goodbye it _was_ worthwhile my coming back like that yesterday wasn't it?
Oh its so lucky as you know I never expected to be able to see the baba and never thought I would be able to see you again before I went off – so we must count our blessings as usual and not mind quite so much if I am not able to be there when it does arrive. Don't worry over me I will come back to you all – I swear I will. I was miserable on my beastly motor bicycle. I hope the baba may have arrived by Thursday morning.
I think the invasion is going jolly well –far better really than I ever thought.
Bless you darling and may God take care of you in my absence.'

This surprise visit was the last that my father was able to make before he left and the last occasion when he could be with my mother and sisters. I would not be born until the 22nd June, some days after he had gone.

There are two more letters that were written in ink dated June 15th which presumably were sent from their camp in England as the Battalion prepared to embark for France. One refers to items of his kit as well as his continuing concerns about the arrival of the baby:

'Here is a lot of junk that I don't want to destroy because it might be useful if and when I go to the Staff again so I might write for it but it is of no conceivable use to me just now (I have his briefcase in front of me as I write – author's note). Also my address book and cheque book. I wish you had been able to produce MJ before this because you must be so bored with all this hanging about.'

and the other that:

'I feel in very close touch with you having seen you so recently and being able to ring up as often as I do.'

My father's remaining letters are written in pencil when he was on the move and in ink when in camp either still in England or when he had arrived in Normandy and was already in the field.

He did not land on D-Day itself but was part of the re-enforcement of the bridgehead on the Normandy coast that began immediately afterwards and continued for many weeks until over 1 million men had arrived in Normandy. Between 6th June and 18th June, when the great storm broke, men arrived into the Mulberry artificial harbour area which covered over 1400 acres. Two long pontoons reached out from the shore into the harbour with a cross piece to which the shipping was tied up. Disembarkation was on foot with vehicles being driven off onto the beach at Arromanche. The remains of the harbour can still be seen today at low tide.

The storm that began on the 18th June almost wrecked the harbour so that the landing of troops was much delayed over the following week.

On the 18th June my father wrote:

'Who would have thought that on June 18th I would still be in England and you would still not have produced Michael John. Somehow just now I am less interested in its sex and more in knowing that both you and him are alright. I feel already out of even the last 5 war years and miles away from our life before that. I believe so because nothing except the affairs of the Regiment and of one's Company. One's horizon's are clamped down to NIL. This time last week I was motorcycling madly to see you. It really was lucky getting that day and having the pony.'

The child had still not been born by the following day and on the 20th my father wrote his final letter in England to remind my mother of the arrangements that he had made for the news to reach him after he had sailed:

'John Vigor came down yesterday. He has a Staff job which involves being able to use a wireless set across the Channel so I think he is probably a better bet even than Kenneth all the more since he knows this Regiment. To confirm what I said (the way my mother should get the news of my birth to him on the frontline – author's note) his telephone is Salisbury 4251 Ext 137. My thoughts are all with you at Sonning and dear God how I wish I was with you.'

From their camp outside Eastbourne the Battalion moved into a marshalling area at Tilbury and there it was split up into two parties for the crossing. The first party was carried in an American vessel, the SS Fort Finlay, which sailed on the 18th but was then held up for three days off Southend due to the bad weather and did not arrive on the beachhead until the 22nd. It then moved to the Guards Armoured Division concentration area outside Bayeux on the 23rd. The second party was carried in an American LST (Landing Ship Transport) that sailed on the 22nd and arrived without incident on the 23rd across almost dry beaches before also moving to Bayeux. My father travelled in the latter.

On the afternoon of the 23rd June the 32nd Guards Brigade, of which the Battalion formed a part alongside the 3rd Irish Guards and the 5th

Coldstream, was detached from the Division and moved forward to take up position at Bretteville L'Orgueilleuse under the command of 43rd Wessex Division. Battalion HQ was located in the orchard of the grounds of a chateau which was used as the officers mess and good trenches were taken over from Canadian troops of the Regina Rifles. This move was in preparation for the start of a battle which was to lead to my father's death.

His last letters were written between the 24th and 27th June from this location and were numbered 1 to 3 on the envelopes. The first was dated 24th before the news of my arrival had reached him.

'I am quite certain that by now your baba has arrived and I am so wanting to know whether it all went well. I hope that you were able to get through to Kenneth or John Vigor or both. We had a very easy voyage and no trouble of any sort. The arrangements were very good and well made and in a fortnight's time or so I shall be able to tell you about it all in more detail. The much vaunted West Wall did not appear formidable at all. There were no roadblocks – no mines and I only saw one strong point. The villages near to the coast look as if they had had an air raid but are no means knocked flat and far less damage than one would suppose and inland are not touched at all.

We are in typical Norman country just as I remember it from the time we came to Caen as children very pretty with masses of little orchards . The French at any rate outside the towns are very friendly and lend the men washing bowls and let them use the pumps and so on. They say that they were short of meat, only had 1 lb of sugar a month and hardly any butter but they don't look any different to what they always looked – all have flash aluminium bicycles and double breasted sports coats or those ridiculous motor bicycles with pedals. Apparently they never saw a German hereabouts until a month ago and then the German troops, although they had good German NCOs, were mostly Russians and Poles. They did not fight here at all but ran away and there are absolutely no signs of fighting whatsoever except for a few slit trenches here and there and the remains of a battle down the road. Some of the Company were thrilled to find some German rifles and helmets in a wood not far away. There are continually our aeroplanes overhead. I have not seen a single German one although at night the AA (Anti-aircraft guns) fire from time to time. We have the guns up at the front generally only at night time. I live perpetually in a girl guide camp atmosphere with little billy cans cooking this and that. We have the inevitable white dog, rather a sweet one that Ginnie would like.

By the 25th he had received the news for which he had been so keenly waiting:

'I don't remember ever having been so happy or so pleased. I got the news via the Guards Armd. Div. today so it did not take very long. Like you I was absolutely thrilled. I think its brilliantly clever of you. I wonder what he looks like and I would love to see him. I can hardly wait to hear all details and the weight and all that sort of thing. I am trying to get a message back to you but if it does not come when you get this letter you will know that I have known very quickly about it. Everyone here has been very nice about it and have been pleased for me. I can't write more I've sent you all my other news yesterday. I'm sitting in front of my tent in the sun with the wireless on and am just about to eat a trout that a soldier gave me having blown it up in the river with a grenade! All my thoughts are with you and my spirit is with you at home.'

On the 27th he wrote his third and final letter. This was the last occasion on which my mother would hear from him:

'I had the most appalling luck yesterday my jeep arrived at long last and had got stuck in the water getting off the ship. It got completely submerged in 30 mins under the waves with the result that all my bedding clothes and everything were just soaking. Actually it might have been a little worse as Davies (my father's soldier servant) had waterproofed the bed roll very well and that wasn't too bad but my flea bag, pillow, etc were v damp and will remain so as it was salt water for the remainder of the campaign. The floppy bag was not too bad either but all my papers in my tin box were soaking and so on. I took my shirts and pyjamas and so on into the local little town and they are being washed so I hope some day to see them again. But it was maddening wasn't it and was in fact the only vehicle in the whole Battalion to suffer in that way – all the fault of some damn fool of an unloading officer who so the driver says put him straight into a hole and into 5 ft of water. Then typically the weather which has been up to now as hot as hot became thundery and today we have had torrential downpours so that I've really been able to get little dried.

Last night we went fishing with explosives but either there were no fish or we had too little explosives for we got nothing. It was fun though and we drank cider at many of the farms we came to.

You are never very far away from my thoughts. I long to hear all your news and the minutest details about the baba yourself and oh almost everything. All my best love and I'll write again when I can.

PS Send writing paper and envelopes all mine ruined.'

The Battalion remained in the orchards at Bretteville L'Orgueilleuse for five days before being ordered forward to the Front on the afternoon of the 29ᵗʰ June.

Into Battle

The battle in which my father was killed was code-named Operation "Epsom" but is more commonly known as the Battle of the Scottish Corridor because it was fought mainly by troops belonging to the 15ᵗʰ Scottish Division, a formation made up of Highland and Lowland TA infantry battalions. It was also known as the Battle of the Odon River because this was the enemy line that had to be breached in order to gain access to Caen which was the operation's objective.

It was the fiercest battle of the Normandy campaign and caused the highest casualties. It was the battle in which the British infantry was *bloodied* and had to learn the hard lessons required to fight and defeat a determined enemy.

The battle that waged over five days at the end of June 1944 represented the implementation of Montgomery's overall strategy which was to attract the full weight of the enemy onto the Allied troops on the eastern flank and by continual attacks on them to "write down" their strength that would enable the Americans to break out with much less opposition in the west.

The first attempts in the second and third weeks of June had been failures as British armour had been ambushed by veteran German tank crews and brought to a standstill at Tilly and Villers-Bocage. Criticism of Montgomery had begun at SHAEF - where he had never been popular - as he failed to deliver the early success that he had promised and the RAF in particular complained that insufficient ground had been won to move their fighter bases from Britain to airfields in France.

Epsom was supposed to answer Montgomery's critics and to strike the decisive blow that he had always intended.

A number of factors caused the battle to become a vicious and protracted struggle. These included the extreme difficulty of using infantry in the *bocage* where small fields surrounded by high banked hedges and sunken farm roads and tracks provided a series of ideal defensive positions. The open acres that did exist and that could have provided some perspective to the battlefield were full of chest height ripening corn; were easily set alight and provided the enemy with open fields of fire.

The British infantry although fully trained and on their mettle were initially no match for the experienced all-arms German fighting groups. The defenders had been fighting in the front-line for over four years in Russia and elsewhere and their co-ordination was superior. Most critical was the enemy's ability to form a series of lightly held defensive lines that incorporated elements of their infantry, artillery and tank units and enabled them to stay mobile in small numbers.

In the first day of the battle beginning on the 26th June, the British infantry made little impact and were astonished by the ferocity of the defence, particularly in and around the village of Cheux, which was taken and retaken throughout the early stages of the battle. At the crossroads at the centre of the village, where five roads met, British and German tanks and infantry were continually in violent contact and the whole area was under constant shelling and mortar fire. The British tanks got hopelessly stuck in endless traffic jams as they approached Cheux and when they did move went about hull-down and so were unable to communicate with the infantry on the ground around them At night the tanks retreated back to their lines leaving the infantry to manage alone.

However, after a faltering start on the 26th June during which the men of many of the fighting battalions simply went to ground, a narrow "corridor" was pushed forward towards the Odon river crossing and on the 27th June a battalion of Argylls crossed at the bridge at Gavrus onto the far bank and was followed by British armour. Realising that they risked being outflanked at Caen by the Allied armies, Hitler and the German High Command finally appreciated that the invasion in Normandy was the location of the main Allied attack on Europe – and not after all in the Pas de Calais as they had been led to believe - and ordered the main German tank force of over 700 tanks and armoured vehicles up to the Front, including 9, 11*SS*, 12*SS*, Panzer Group Lehr and Das Reich divisions , the latter the butchers of Oradour-sur-Glane, all of which had been held back in the north. They were ordered to move with all speed towards Normandy.

Meanwhile in the *bocage* between Cheux and what was to become known as the Calvary of the high ground of Hill 112 at Esquay a series of fierce actions took place as the British infantry became more proficient and experienced some success in dislodging the enemy. By this time the battle had moved on from the crossroads at Cheux although the enemy had its range and still rained down its artillery and mortar fire whenever the dust from moving vehicles could be observed.

Whilst Montgomery claimed the battle was a success and had helped to suck in and pin down the enemy in just the way that he had intended, the reality was that a relatively thin screen of enemy troops had held down the greatly superior Allied numbers. By the 28th June the pace of the battle was slowing, but the "corridor" was still under sporadic attack and the lodgement on the other side of the Odon was in danger of being surrounded by German tanks and infantry. In four days of intense fighting there had been 10,000, mainly British casualties, of whom 2,500 were dead. The Allied lines were tidied up and the troops beyond the river were withdrawn.

However, this was not quite the end of the battle. On the 29th June, Montgomery's 21st Army headquarters received the first intimation from de-crypted "Ultra" signals that Hitler had released his tank force and that it was racing towards Normandy to destroy the Allied positions between the Norman coast and Caen and hurl the Allies back into the sea.

The End

It was at this moment, on the afternoon of the 29th June and in anticipation of an attack the following day of the whole might of the German armour, that 32nd Guards Brigade was detached from the Guards Armoured Division and instructed to take up defensive positions in and around Cheux to act as a back-stop to whatever might happen next. The First Battalion, Welsh Guards was the leading battalion of the Brigade and took up position SSW of Cheux.

My godfather, Joe Vandeleur commanding 3rd Battalion Irish Guards, takes up the story of the events of the 29th and 30th June:

'Going up the battlefield was the most extraordinary experience. We moved up a road parallel to the coast as far as St Croix. Up to this point there were no signs of war. We turned south and just as if we were walking onto a cinema set, the war struck us bang in the face. First, the appalling smell of death, piles of dead cows lying on their backs with legs stretched out like pokers, German and British tanks blown to pieces, the houses totally destroyed and the ground cut to ribbons by shelling.
The Welsh took up positions covering Cheux and my battalion took up positions between them and the Canadians on the edge of Capriquet aerodrome, which was in the hands of the Germans. The 5th Coldstream protected our right flank and rear. The 15th Scottish Division, supported by an armoured brigade, then began to trickle through Cheux'.

These were the troops moving back from the bridgehead across the Odon.

'The Germans bombarded Cheux with everything they'd got and

started to counter attack with armour. The Jocks had a very nasty approach march and we shared some of the dirt that was being thrown at us '

This was the result of the enemy targeting moving vehicles at the crossroads and the beginning of the German counter-attack as more tanks arrived at the front from the north.

'The Welsh Guards had their Commanding Officer and second-in-command wounded immediately. A very great friend of mine. Johnny Fass took over their command. He sent me a message saying he had some great news. I went over to see him getting thoroughly shelled on the way. I found him in a slit trench with his soldier servant. He showed me a telegram from his wife, saying he had had a son. He asked me to be the godfather. His soldier servant, he and I drank mugs of tea mixed with whisky. I got out of the trench and started to walk home. I had not walked more than a few yards when a mortar bomb landed right in the trench, killing Johnny.' (Vandeleur)

The historian of the Regiment wrote about the move to Cheux on 29th June and my father's death on the 30th:

'The element of chance in warfare was never more clearly illustrated than on their first evening there. The companies were hardly in position and the men of Battalion HQ were still digging-in in their field when they were heavily mortared. The CO, 2ic, Anti-tank gun officer, Signals Officer, a CSM and a number of guardsmen were wounded and had to be evacuated to England. And this was not the end of their misfortune. Major JE Fass who took command was killed the following evening almost in the same place and in the same way. In Lieut-Col Browning, Major Smart and Major Fass the Battalion thus lost its three senior officers.' (Ellis)

George Browning wrote of these events from hospital in Glamorgan after his evacuation to England to Horrie Noble who had made enquires about the details of my father's death:

'We had been in process of taking over on a flank of the gap leading across the river Odon. A Boche counter-attack was in progress on the afternoon of the 29th when we had been doing this. Result we remained doubled with this Bn. The Boche never reached our position and there was probably an observer hidden in a cornfield or somewhere because we kept on getting attacked. Bursts of a few rounds at us from 88 guns and mortars. It was also in the middle of a gun area and the noise was too great to allow us to spot where it was coming from. A crack on Bn HQ caught me, Worrall and Herapath (Sigs Off.) Bn HQ was moved after that to another part of the same field. Next evening at much the same time Johnny had just finished an "O" Group when the same thing happened. He was hit in the head and killed instantly. That is all I know. The Bn. up to 10th July had 8 killed and 50 wounded all from spasmodic shell and mortar fire directed I am certain by some hidden OP. The corn was so long and the country so close that it was impossibly difficult to spot snipers before they had done a lot of damage. BLAST IT!! I am so damned angry and being quite helpless. What is the use!

Tell Liza what I have been told. She has probably heard a firsthand account by now. It was damned good of Johnny to break away from his Staff job!!'

General Alan Adair commanding the Guards Armoured Division commented that the loss of key senior officers was worrying as the Welsh Guards 'had lost their Commanding Officer GW Browning and his successor JE Fass on successive nights due to enemy shelling'.

The Battalion's Intelligence Section sergeant who was an accomplished artist and diarist also wrote of the events of these two days. He was in a good position to do so as the section's truck was always parked close to Battalion HQ. First he described the arrival into their positions:

'We were sent to hold a line behind some newly won ground not yet secure. We had to dig in upon our arrival last evening (29th) and had moved through our own artillery concentration of wheeled guns – a continuous barrage of fire. Then into this field which was full of our 25 pounder guns firing like mad nonstop. Traffic jams on our way down, very unpleasant as enemy shelling increased in volume. The CO said that SS Panzer divisions were counter attacking and urged us to speed our digging. The din was terrific and drowned the noise of German shells and mortars which were landing intermittently in our field, but in the orchards on our right, mortar bombs were falling thickly and regularly about 150 yards away.' (Murrell)

He commented on the men of the 15th Scottish Division who Joe Vandeleur had described as *trickling back* through their lines after the heavy fighting of the previous days which was also described in the Battalion's War Diary for the day 'to add to the confusion, men of an Inf. Div. which had been badly knocked about were withdrawing piecemeal through our position'. The diarist reported:

'Some British soldiers lay huddled against the banks of the road. Two of them lay dead, slain by the mortars. These men looked rough and dazed and seemed to be leaderless. Stragglers from the battle, who had been overrun by 12th SS Panzer Division tanks and by Panzer Grenadiers. Presumably all their officers and NCOs were killed or wounded and they could go no further. The horror of their experience was obvious in the their eyes.' (Murrell)

As darkness fell on the 29th the situation became even more tense and as George Browning had noted *there was probably an observer hidden in a cornfield or somewhere and shell and mortar fire directed I am certain by some hidden OP* (author's italics):

'Meanwhile it grew dark. The SP (self-propelled) guns in our field suddenly ceased their hectic shooting, packed up and retired through our lines. An ominous sign that heralded the near-approach of the German Panzers. Machine gun tracer bullets seemed to be coming from a corner of our field on a fixed line. We suspected that this might be a guide to Jerry's mortars and Arty.' (Murrell)

It was now that George Browning's HQ was hit and he and others were killed or wounded. As a precaution Battalion HQ was moved and my father took command of the Battalion.

During the following day, the 30th, some re-organisation took place and

General Adair came up to make a morale raising visit and confirm my father in his appointment.

By evening the Battalion was once again preparing itself to meet the counter-attack of the Panzer divisions on Cheux and the Scottish Corridor now reckoned to consist of over 700 tanks in number. The expected attack did not materialise but:

> 'The deepest penetration of the enemy had now reached a point only just the other side of the woods and orchard that were so liberally mortared and shelled and only a few hundred yards from Battalion HQ. The Germans must have come through the woods and debouched from it at the point where Battalion HQ lay. It is the focal point in the salient for German guns.' (Murrell)

And as night drew on:

> 'German shell and mortar fire was stepped up to an almost continual bombardment as heavy and protracted as the previous night's shelling. Many shells landed on us from the newly arrived Panzer divisions – mostly 88s and 105s but there were mortar bombs too. There was a particularly spiteful burst of hate. Battalion HQ was being pasted.' (Murrell)

It was at this moment, as my father sheltered in his personal trench with his soldier servant, Davies, that he was killed instantly by shell or mortar fire:

> 'It was dark but in the area of battalion HQ it was black. The shells had created a black cloud of dust and pungently acrid smell through which dimly-seen figures ran to and fro and men shouted for stretcher bearers and orders mingled with the cries of badly hurt men.' (Murrell)

He was gone. G-o-n-e-a-w-a-y – G-o-n-e a-w-a-y!

Chapter Eleven
EPILOGUE

Let us remember those who will not come back: their constancy and courage in battle, their sacrifice and endurance in the face of a merciless enemy.
(HM King George VI in a radio broadcast on VE Day 8th May 1945)

News from France

The first intimation of my father's death was given in a letter written by Oliver *'Nod'* Wrightson, his first cousin and the youngest of the Wrightson boys, on the night of his death. It was not, of course received in England until early July (probably around the 7th). Casualty figures in Normandy were mounting at an alarming rate by the end of June and were not usually released for at least two weeks. The letter reads:

'Friday night, June 30th
Lt O. Wrightson
Coldstream Guards
HQ 32nd Guards Brigade

Dear Lisa,
It's nearly an hour since I started to write this letter, and I still can't think how I can properly convey what I feel to you.
We heard the frightful news at 9.50 this evening in the Mess tent, and no one spoke for at least three minutes. Everyone here was devoted to Johnnie, and its been the most terrible blow to all of us....
I saw Johnny only this morning, when he had taken over command of the Battalion, and there was the most complete confidence in

him. He was incredibly popular with everyone and his loss is quite incalculable.'

He also wrote to my grandmother Fass, my father's mother, at the same time and along similar lines but added:

'He was killed absolutely instantaneously, no possibility of any pain.'

and he wrote to my mother again in July:

'I heard from someone in his company that he did definitely get your letter telling him all about Michael John on either the 28th or 29th. Things were so hectic from the 27th to the 30th that he couldn't possibly have been able to write a reply. Also, I talked to Michael Ling last night who had been within 30m yards of him at the time and he's going to write to you.'

Michael Ling then wrote:

'You cannot need to be told what a quite terrible loss his death was. He had been back in the battalion such a very short time that when both the commanding officer and Maurice Smart were both wounded the night before, it was a very great responsibility for Johnny so suddenly to find himself in command of the Bn. But it was an even greater tragedy that he had only one day in which to hold a command which he would have done so very well. For very certainly we all had the fullest and greatest confidence in him. I don't know if you have had any details but it was late in the evening and Johnny had spent the day going around and seeing various "high-ups" that he knew and he had called us together for a conference to tell us what he had learned about the general situation. He had just finished giving us an extremely good talk when two or three German mortar bombs fell out of the blue straight onto battalion headquarters. Johnny was hit and without any question died quite painlessly and instantaneously. (14/07/1944)

Joe Vandeleur confirmed the way my father died when he wrote the following day:

'Your poor dear Johnnie was killed <u>outright</u> by a shell at 10.15pm yesterday evening. He was commanding and was so happy about you and his son. He had asked me to be godfather. His past hours with us were so happy. Now we all grieve for you and the children. We all miss Johnny so much and his gay way. There was not an instants pain and he left this world so gay.' (01/07/1944)

and a friend of my mother's wrote from the American Ambulance:

'I moved a man today who was actually with Johnny when he was killed. He assured me that it was absolutely instantaneous. He seemed a most awfully nice man and before I said that I was any connection of Johnny's was full of what a "first rate chap" he was. I think he had been a PT instructor in Johnny's battalion.' (23/08/1944)

The padre to the First Battalion, Padre Payne, wrote:

'I buried him in a little plot with some other Welsh guardsmen. He was killed instantly and did not suffer.'
(04/07/1944)

My mother used the idea of the complete confidence in which my father was held by the whole Battalion that had been referred to by both Oliver Wrightson and Michael Ling when she wrote to her brother Michael in August:

'He planned the whole invasion and then when it was ready said he must go and take part in it. The guardsmen thought the world of him and when he got command said apparently that "he was where he belonged and would lead them to success".

A friend wrote that such was his popularity that the news of his death was known throughout the <u>Army</u> within 3 hours of it happening.'

Another of his Company officers, Eddie Bedingfeld, also referred to the days shortly before he was killed:

'He died without suffering and had been on top of his form after the news of Michael John's arrival. That had made him very happy and he often used to talk with me in the evenings of you and the children. I have visited his grave and found it in good order with some lovely white lilies on it which had been out there by some of the guardsmen,

It was a very great shock to us to lose him so soon after taking over the Bn and I personally felt it very keenly as I had seen so much of him lately and had got to know him really well.

We all had great confidence in his leadership and hopes for the future. Pray for us that we may do well in battle and come through with honour and achievement.' (27/07/1944)

My mother must have had the news on or around the 7th July and this happened in at least two ways. First, my Verey grandfather went to lunch at his London club and an acquaintance with connections in the War Office came up to him and told him how sorry he was to hear that my father, his son in law, had been killed. It was the first my grandfather knew of it and he took the next train from Paddington down to Twyford, told his wife, got out his car and drove the short distance to Sonning to give my mother the dreadful news. It must have been a ghastly moment for both of them.

Second, Horace 'Horrie' Noble at HQ London District heard the news at about the same time and wrote to my mother on the 10th and 12th July. He wished my mother to know more about the circumstances of my father's death and was in communication with George Browning who had been evacuated to hospital in Wales and whose description of the events of 29th/30th June has been detailed in the previous chapter. Horrie wrote:

'10 July 44

Liza Dear,
I am trying to get amplification from Regt. HQ but this has not come

through yet, they told me today...but you have my lasting affection and deep sympathy. Sympathy which as you know is derived from my love for Johnny, and is therefore very real. It is not for me to tell you what a wonderful personality and charm Johnny had...but I do want you know that I thought he was the nicest and most loyal friend I ever had. His going back to regimental duty when there was no necessity for him to do so was typical of the man...Such a wonderful example of all that is best in human nature will always live in the hearts of those, like myself, who had the honour of his friendship. But for Johnny I would give this thought that *all the trumpets sounded for him on the other side'.*

On the 12th July he wrote again:

'Liza Dear,
George Browning, as you know, was wounded and is in hospital at Penarth, Glamorgan...if you would like to get into touch with him. I saw John Vigor last night, who told me he had seen Johnny the day before he left. He got his old company back, with practically the same men as he had before. He commanded the Battalion before he was killed, which must have made him very proud, and he was cheerful and gallant to the end.

By the 15th July the news was made official and an announcement was placed in the Times newspaper to that effect:

'FASS, - In June 1944, while commanding his battalion, Lt-Col JOHN FASS, Welsh Guards, most beloved husband of Elizabeth, of Pound Cottage, Sonning, Berks, and dearly loved only son of Sir Ernest and Lady Fass of Foxhill, Inkpen, Berks. Aged 33.

Legends of the Home Front

My mother used to tell two stories about what happened at the time of my father's death which one might describe as *legends.* Both were recounted to her by individuals who claimed to have special powers of sight - not necessarily wholly fictitious.

My father had arranged for some extra help for my mother to look after me and my sisters after I was born and she was responsible for some night-time duties. In the middle of the night of the 30th – the night my father was killed - she entered the temporary night nursery in which I lay in my cot to check that I was alright and found a man dressed in khaki battledress and wearing boots and gaiters, leaning over the cot and looking in at me. As the door opened he turned towards it and was gone.

On the following day - the afternoon of the 1st July – my Fass grandmother was sitting in her parlour that overlooked the front drive, reading the newspaper after lunch. The parlour's window looked directly up the drive towards the open gate that was not more than thirty paces away. For some reason she glanced up and saw that a woman dressed in grey had come through the gate and was standing a short distance up the drive where she was picking a bunch of flowers from the nearest border in the garden. My grandmother dropped the newspaper she was holding, left the parlour, went through the Hall and opened the front door. She advanced up the drive intent on asking the woman what she was doing picking the flowers! As she reached the woman, the woman turned towards her with a sad look on her face and presented her with the bunch. At that moment my grandmother knew that my father was dead.

Character & Condolences

Horrie Noble –perhaps with the help of Jock Whitefoord, for whom my father had worked at COSSAC - had also started work on the draft for an Obituary that would appear in the Times in early August. This would read:

'Lieut-Colonel John Fass. Welsh Guards
A brother officer writes:

The Army has lost a first class officer and leader in Johnny Fass, killed in action in command of his Battalion, and his many friends feel a sad blank without his engaging and attractive personality.
Johnny Fass radiated vitality, energy and enthusiasm – for soldiering and life in general. I only had the privilege of knowing him in wartime, but saw the sterling work he did as an operational staff officer with formations training at home. And subsequently how he

186

filled a very responsible position as a First Grade Staff Officer at Supreme Headquarters with very great success.

Posted to a Staff appointment as a Lieut-Colonel where there was little chance of active service, he begged to go back to command a company in his Regiment. . Within a few weeks he had been given command of his Battalion, only to be killed just as he had attained his ambition to see service.

Johnny Fass would have gone far – in the Army or in any sphere of activity where his drive could have made a mark.

Johnny was the embodiment of loyalty to his superiors. His personality made him equally popular with colleagues and subordinates and he had the knack of getting the very best out of his staff. Johnny was the happy warrior who lived his life to the full and at work and play – and all his friends will sadly miss his laughter and gaiety, whether soldiering, hunting, shooting or just enjoying his company.'

Over the following weeks and months my mother received many letters from brother officers with whom my father had served both pre- and during the war, including a number whom she had never met. In addition, there were many letters from their joint friends and relatives as well as a number from those who had already suffered widowhood themselves.

My mother's heart must have been doubly pierced: She had lost the husband who she had adored at the same time as having to nurse their new born child in her arms and she would be haunted by the memory of this time - and of their lives together - for the rest of her life.

The letters confirmed the words that Horrie and Jock wished to use in their Obituary. Jock wrote from West Africa where he was serving with the West African forces as Chief of Staff:

'You know how fond I was of Johnny and how much I thought of him – as a friend and the most loyal staff officer I have ever had the luck to serve with. I feel that you must think bitterly that if he had not been too loyal to me – he would never have been commanding his Bn. – but I had hoped he would be spared to make his mark in the field as I knew he would. I have taken the liberty to try and write an appreciation of Johnny in case you and Sir Ernest and Lady Fass would care for an appreciation to appear in the Times I should like to make a public tribute to Johnny's qualities as a soldier and as a friend.' (29/07/1944)

as did Jock's wife Molly:

'Jock will be very sad when he gets my air mail letter, he was so very fond of Johnny and valued his never failing loyalty and cheerful friendliness as much as he appreciated his able co-operation all the time they worked together. It is a sad blow for all Johnny's friends who will miss him terribly.' (17/07/1944)

My father's Aunt Gwen Wrightson wrote from Neasham where he had spent so much time as a young man in the company of his cousins and best friend Peter Wrightson:

'Dear Johnnie, how I loved him more like a 5th son than just a nephew. He was always welcome here and I think he knew it. He used to come breezing in just like a tonic shouting at the top of his voice "Auntie Gwen".
I want to tell you what Nod wrote. I got it today – "July 1st I'm afraid I've got some very bad news for you. Johnnie has just been killed. It happened at 10pm last night and we heard a minute later from the Welsh over the wireless. We were all in the Mess tent and no one spoke for at least 4 minutes. Johnnie had only just heard that Liza had given him a son. He was instantaneously killed – no pain. It's a very great blow to everyone here and at home." (07/07/1944)

and later in July:

'He was so vital and radiant and such an absolute darling. Everyone loved him here. (18/07/1944)

The eldest of the Wrightson boys, my father's cousin John, wrote:

'I was at Brigade Headquarters last Saturday and saw Nod who told me that Johnnie had just taken over command of his regiment that day. I feel he died as he would have liked knowing that you had just presented him with a son and that he had just got command of his regiment. I remember the last time I saw him he was very unhappy in his liaison job with the Poles and was doing all he could to get back to the regiment. Nod said he was a pillar of strength to his chaps and I can only too well believe it.

What fun we used to have with him particularly when he was up at Catterick before the war and used to come over to Eryholme. And then later on at Neasham.

During the war I have been lucky to have seen quite a lot of him. What fun we had last summer when I came over to Sonning. He was always such a tonic whenever I met him; however depressed I was, he always cheered me up. And all his friends found the same infectious spirit.

I hope you will understand how you are not alone in missing one who was a friend who could always be relied on and who was always cheerful and happy.' (12/07/1944)

My mother invited Robby Lawrence to visit her at Sonning to see her and the baby and she wrote afterwards:

'Johnny was such a wonderful person and made a year of my ATS life more fun than anyone else could have. I went down yesterday and saw Jimmie Ames and Kenneth Burda, they were, as I expected, terribly upset. I have written off today to General Jock – I don't know how long it will take to get there.' (12/07/1944)

Kenneth Burda who had shared a flat with my father whilst they were both working at Norfolk House wrote from SHAEF:

'Johnny was, to me, a very splendid person because, although he was my master, he was also someone on whose friendship I could have relied for many years to come. There is a tremendous sense of loss here among those who worked and laughed with him in the early days of the Headquarters. There is a very real admiration for Johnny, who had the courage to leave a job when he thought fit and to see the thing through on the battlefield.' (10/07/1944)

Tony McComas , another officer from the same headquarters wrote of their days at COSSAC:

'Words are inadequate to express one's admiration and appreciation of such a delightful person but I should like you to know how sincerely the sympathies of all of us who worked with him are with you at the moment.

Johnnie was so very popular here both as an officer and an individual and I personally feel that I have lost a most charming and helpful friend.

His personality and perpetual cheerfulness were sadly missed when he left and all of us took a great interest in his future which was obviously going to be a successful one.

I am so glad to hear from Robby Lawrence that she has been down to see you as she is such a kind sympathetic person.

Gen Whitely has asked me to express to you his deepest sympathy. He feels that as he does not know you it would be kinder not to burden you with another letter but I know that he had the highest opinion and regard for Johnnie.'
(07/07/1944)

A family friend in Berkshire wrote about my father's contribution to the work of COSSAC:

'A relative of ours in Intelligence was here when we heard about John. "Not Johnnie Fass, I hope, he has done brilliantly – such good work and so charming."
(15/07/1944)

Gill Gambier Parry, an ATS in SHAEF's Intelligence Division wrote about the Norfolk House days from the point of view of the office staff:

'You won't know who I am but I worked for him at Norfolk House for some months and all of us who were there were horrified to hear the news.

It is little consolation I know to tell you how many people have said such nice things about Johnny – right down to his orderlies. We all knew he would have no regard for his own self when it came to it. Working for him was terrific fun, if not always very easy! But he was a wonderful 'master' and certainly trained me very strictly for which I shall always be grateful'. (18/07/1944)

and General FE *Monkey* Morgan, the architect of *Overlord* now Chief of Staff at SHAEF, wrote:

'Those of us who remain from the Norfolk House days of last year miss your Johnny sadly.' (10/09/1944)

Elizabeth Serecold, a friend of my mother's who had worked at Norfolk House and was now at SHAEF also wrote about COSSAC days:

'he enjoyed living so much and was therefore a delightful person to be with. He was much missed when he left the office and everybody who had worked with him was fond of him. He was one of the most popular people here. I was so glad for him to hear that he had got back to regimental duty and was commanding his battalion. It must have been so exciting to have planned the operation and then put it into effect. ' (21/07/1944)

Brigadier George Johnson, commanding 32nd Guards Brigade wrote:

'Though I don't know you I feel I must write as Johnnie's brigadier to say how very distressed we all are. He had just got his chance to command his battalion and would I know have done it with great success. I can assure you that his service has not been wasted as in his previous capacity he had done a very great job towards improving and maintaining the efficiency of his battalion. A cruel accident of war deprived him the chance of leading it. I send my deepest sympathy and that of all at brigade headquarters.' (05/07/1944)

His friend Rowley Errington, the Staff Captain from 33rd Guards Brigade now promoted to Major, wrote from HQ, Guards Armoured Division:

'He died in the way I think he would have wished, commanding a battalion of his regiment and I have a feeling that if it had got to happen that would have been Johnny's choice.

In my soldiering career I have never met anyone with whom I would rather serve. It is a most terrible loss to you and an irreplaceable loss to all of his friends of whom, he had a multitude, amongst whom I like to think I was one. I will never forget all the kindness he showed me in his always cheerful way. (02/07/1944)

as did Norman Railing another officer from the 33rd Guards Brigade days:

'I was very fond of Johnnie and shall always remember him as one of the most charming people I've ever had the good fortune to meet'. (15/07/1994)

and Rupert Hart-Davis a wartime commissioned officer of the Coldstream also from 33rd Brigade:

'You couldn't know him without loving him. He was so tremendously alive and gay and helpful and friendly. I shall always remember his kindness and assistance to me in 33rd Guards Brigade. He was a magnificent soldier, and, unlike so many regular soldiers, he was human and understanding towards temporary soldiers like myself. Also, of course, it is right-thinking people like him that we shall need after the war. My beloved Col Bunty Stewart Brown was killed just after Johnny. They liked each other a lot. Let's hope they're laughing together somewhere.' (25/08/1944)

The head of the Home Guard in whose sector the 33rd Guards Brigade operated wrote:

'When the 33rd Guards Brigade were stationed in my sector we saw a good deal of him and held him in high regard for his charming personality and soldierly qualities'. (19/07/1994)

Colonel Bankier, the Colonel commanding the Regiment, wrote from Headquarters, Welsh Guards:

'I have known Johnnie well throughout the war and our paths have crossed many times. A more charming, delightful and efficient officer could not be found and when his chance came, it seems just too cruel that fate took the course it did. The Regiment, who have been hard hit in the last few weeks, could ill afford such a loss.
I have promised to let your father know at once any further news I may receive.' (12/07/1944)

Henry Carden, a Lieut-Colonel serving in Normandy with HQ 2 Armoured Replacement Group, and an old army friend with whom he had been at school, wrote to my mother about the news having been known throughout the army to which she referred later in her letter to her brother Michael:

'I am so sorry, and I can only say that this is a general remark throughout the army here. Johnnie's popularity was such that the news of his death was known everywhere within 3 or 4 hours. It cast a great glory on his many friends and he had no enemies.' (03/07/1944)

Herbert Lloyd Johnson An officer of the British Liaison HQ in Edinburgh wrote:

'On behalf of all ranks of this HQ I am writing to say how shocked we all are to hear of Johnnie's death in action. Our very deep sympathy in your great loss. Johnny was a born leader and I am glad to see he was commanding his battalion at the last. We were all very fond of him here and I am sure his time here was happy one. His death is a great loss to us all and I feel he would have gone a long way in the years to come.' (15/07/1944)

as did the Chief of Staff, First Polish Army Corps Chief of Staff, Colonel Wieckowski:

'I had the honour to work with Lt. Col. Fass during his attachment to No. 4 Liaison Headquarters. We all liked him very much indeed, because he was very good soldier, a nice gentleman and a good friend.' (30/07/1944)

Another officer at British Liaison HQ rote:

'It seems a very short time since he left Edinburgh and we had sadly said goodbye to him from No. 4 Liaison where he had done us and our allies no end of good by his energy and enormous charm. From a military point of view I fear his vitality was considered wasted up here and I am so glad to see that he came to command his battalion,' (24/07/1944)

Another of my father's flatmates from Norfolk House days wrote:

'I was hoping that later news might come through that it wasn't true. It seems impossible to be true. I did enjoy knowing him so much, and that time we had in the flat together was really the greatest fun in the world. And in the office we were always ringing each other up and holding impossible conversations. Incidentally he was a very good staff officer and made a very considerable success of the Intelligence work he was doing. Everyone was very fond of him here of course and it has been a great shock to everyone. I heard from him only a fortnight ago.'

In mid-July George Browning, who had been wounded and evacuated the previous night to my father's death, and who had already written to Horrie about its circumstances, now wrote to my mother:

'Unfortunately I can tell you nothing about the circumstances because I don't know. I was hit in the evening of the 29th (I think) and went back on a stretcher that night to a dressing station thinking that I had left the battalion in the hands of Maurice Smart. To my astonishment I discovered Maurice also wounded on a stretcher beside me. He had been hit at the same time as me and I never knew it. So Johnny was left in command – I believe it was the next day the 30th that Johnny was hit. I imagine it must have been by a burst of mortar or shellfire like that which caught me. Or it may have been a sniper of which there were a few about. But I really do not know and I am anxiously waiting for details. We were not really fighting at the time which makes it all the more tiresome.. Just being shelled occasionally.

I can say this. It was absolutely splendid of Johnny to come back to the Regiment from a staff job, taking a lower rank and the obvious risks when he need not have done so. I only wish that he and I had been lucky enough to have a chance of seeing it through together. The regiment has every reason to be proud of him and his loss is a matter which takes away from us not only an extremely efficient officer but such a delightful and damned good brother officer. (12/07/1944)

George's brother Bill also in the Regiment wrote:

'We shall all miss Johnny terribly. He was beloved by all in the Regiment who were fortunate enough to soldier with him. Only recently I wrote to Johnny congratulating him on his son. I feel his loss keenly. He was such a vital and utterly delightful person to be with. I have lost a friend and the Regiment one of their best officers.' (18/07/1944)

Nigel Fisher, who had been trained by my father in the early days of the war and was now serving as a Captain in the 2nd (Armoured) Battalion, Welsh Guards in Normandy wrote:

'I heard the news as soon as it happened, but could not write sooner as we are not allowed to mention casualties until a fortnight afterwards or until they are announced in the Press. It was the most terrible shock to us all in this Bn, and especially to me of everyone here I knew Johnnie best and was most fond of him. It is still almost incredible that it could have happened. Just a stray shell or mortar bomb – I do not know which.

I had not seen Johnnie but have been over to the Bn since and I have had a talk with Cyril (Heber-Percy) who is now commanding. He told me this that, after George Browning and Maurice Smart were wounded, Johnnie took over. That he was wonderfully calm and steady and had a complete grip of the whole situation. His orders were first class, in Cyril's opinion, which is well worth having in these things as he is a very fine officer himself.

Johnnie would have made a very great success in command. I am sure you will have something from others in that Bn. He only held command for one day and was killed the following night. He was such a splendid person – kind and gay and such a good friend. It is so hard that it should have been him when he had so much to live for and was looking forward so much to the time when the war would be over and he would be with you and the children and his many friends.

One thing you will like to know that he knew about the baby at least I am sure he must have done because I saw John Vigor just before I left England which was two or three days later than Johnnie and he told me he had sent the news for him by some special method of communication he had owing to his job. So he will have been happy in that knowledge.' (11/07/1944)

Later Nigel went on to fight with the Guards Armoured Division at the disastrous battle of Arnhem - the dash for the bridges across the Rhine in Holland – and won an MC for bravery whilst attempting to cross the bridge at Nijmegen. After the war he became a Conservative MP and was latterly Father of the House of Commons.

John Vigor also wrote about the receipt of the message:

'I saw him in the marshalling area the day before the Battalion embarked and saw him quite a lot about that time. I had your message about the birth of your son sent off by teleprint from Command HQ so he knew practically the same time as they landed in France or very shortly afterwards.' (16/08/1944)

A colleague from the Home Guard who my father had probably met at 33rd Brigade wrote:

'I found him one of the most charming and helpful of young men I had ever met and all who knew him were sure that he had a brilliant career before him.

and Major Philip Hight, my father's commanding officer from the Royal Berkshire Regiment's Depot days at Brock Barracks in Reading wrote:

'From the time I had Johnny as my Adjutant at the Regimental Depot

I knew he would go far and I am sure he would have risen to the top of the tree. I look back upon very pleasant memories of Johnny as a loyal friend and an extremely efficient soldier who was very popular with officers and men alike. His loss is indeed irreplaceable to you whilst the Army and the Nation have lost one of their very best sons.' (17/07/1944)

as did Brigadier Pendlebury of 225 Brigade, my father's first commanding officer after he left Staff College, whose son, Michael, had just been killed:

'I felt Johnny's loss deeply – I admired him so much, not only because he was such a brilliant staff officer, but also because of his unfailing high spirits and good humour. Like Michael he had a wonderful zest for life. The country can ill spare such gallant youth.' (07/06/1945)

Others wrote:

'Johnny was one of the very best. He must have had countless friends as no one could help liking him and he was always such fun'.

'Your husband was such a charming vital man, so full of the joys of life'.

'We did so admire his huge enthusiasm for everything he was doing coupled with his delightful sense of humour about it all. You must be proud of the way he did his work and particularly of his determined return to regimental duty for the invasion, when he was intended to remain a Lieut.-Col at home for bit longer.'

'Johnnie was so right to go with the regiment and I feel sure his men appreciated that but the outcome is very hard for you and the children.'

'I shall always remember Johnny as one of the most charming people I have ever met.'

'He achieved his ambition of every regular soldier that I have met, that is to lead his battalion in action. Knowing him I am quite sure that he led them well. He could not have done more.'

'Johnny was the dearest of friends and this news is the saddest of the whole war. In a report on him that I saw, it said that he could be relied on to do a good job and enjoy doing it. They could not have given him better or truer praise.' (17/07/1944)

'I suppose it was a case of the old story – the regular soldier pulling every possible string to get back to his men. Well, Johnny did and fell, I hope, as he would have wished but it is desperately cruel on you and the children.' (16/07/1944)

'I never saw much of Johnny but I liked him immensely – as did everyone I have ever met, who knew him. He was so gay and charming.' 15/07/1944)

'Johnnie I am sure would have gone a long way as he had every quality of a soldier and was a loyal and charming friend.' 16/07/1944)

'Johnnie was a great man and a good friend. Perhaps I, who knew him probably as well as most in the Regiment, am qualified to tell you what an enormous loss was sustained by not only the Regiment but by all who knew him. A better friend or man to serve with couldn't be found.' (21/08/1944)

'It was such a grand thing your husband did in leaving a safe staff job to go and fight.' (11/07/1944)

'Johnny was such a great man and if it is any consolation to you there is no one who will not deplore his loss from the service.' (04/08/1944)

The last word on character and of condolence should go to a lifelong family friend of both my mother and father and of my sisters, myself and, latterly, my children. Effie Barker was a near neighbour to Bridge House, my mother's home at Twyford, who lived at Stanlake Park. She was the youngest child by many years to her older brothers and had been brought up with the three Verey children as her French mother was my grandmother's best friend.

She was a keen horsewoman and had got to know my father when he was a young man out hunting with Mr Garth's hounds in East Berkshire before the war and during it when he could snatch a day in the field. Effie wrote:

'Alas, there is nothing that I can say to you and on these occasions words are but meaningless symbols without shadow or substance. Yet they are the only coin we can use to pay tribute to the memory of one who in his person included all the most attractive qualities that can be found in mankind – kindness of heart, infinite courage, good humour and a light gaiety that was like a glass of champagne to all who came his way. There are few people who possessed such boundless charm as did Johnnie and this I think will remain in everyone's memory as a unique quality – something that brought a feeling of warmth and comfort to each person he met during the course of the day. You will as usual face life with a smile which is I am certain the most precious tribute you can pay to the memory of one whose expression never wore a frown' (06/07/1944)

In 1949 the West Downs Memorial to the boys who had been killed in the First Great war was re-dedicated with the addition of the eighty-two old boys who had been killed between 1939-1945. At the ceremony which my mother attended with her parents, Lieut.-General Sir Frederick *'Boy'* Browning, an *OWD*, commander of the British Airborne Corps during the war and a Grenadier guardsman, gave the address in which he said:

'We have, for our numbers, sustained heavy loss. We can all remember those many boys with whom we were brought up here, all of them with such promise in their lives, with whom we never had the opportunity of fulfilling a lifetime's friendship and who themselves were denied a full span of years. Those who died for us in the firm belief that they were fighting for the preservation of decency, honesty and the hopeful future of the world are not to be mourned in sorrow and with regret. Their sacrifice should be remembered with pride, gratitude and courage.' (Hitchens)

Who is John Fass?

After my mother's death, aged 92, in 2002 my sister Serena arranged for a memorial plaque to my father to be erected in the Welsh Guards side-chapel in the Guards Chapel on Birdcage Walk. The original Chapel had received a direct hit from a flying bomb on the 18th June 1944 just before my father crossed to France. There had been over 600 casualties as the morning service had been in progress and the chapel had been packed with the families and friends of those serving in the Guards Armoured Division about to cross to France. It was restored and re-opened by HM The Queen in 1964. My mother had attended that ceremony and after she was re-widowed always went to the Welsh Guards Remembrance Sunday service held at the Chapel.

On this occasion, the family was seated near the front and a brief dedication of my father's memorial was conducted by the chaplain to the Household Division. As it concluded I heard a voice in the pew behind me say quite loudly "Who is John Fass?". I turned around to see who it was who had spoken and my eye rested on a sandy-haired, reddish-faced, 50-ish retired officer of the Regiment.

Well, he knows now!

Hwy clod na hoedl

BIBLIOGRAPHY

Note: Authors quoted directly in the book are marked *

*Adair A (1986). *A Guards' General,* Hamish Hamilton, London, ISBN 0-241-11947-2

*Allport A (2015), *Browned Off & Bloody-Minded,* Yale University Press, New Haven, ISBN 978-0-300-17075-7

*Beevor A (2009), *D-Day,* Penguin, London, ISBN 978-0-670-88703-3

*Blight G (1953), *The Royal Berkshire Regiment 1920-1947,* Staples, London

*Cromer E (1991), *From This Day Forward,* Harmsworth, Stoke Abbott, ISBN 0948807-1-48

Danchev A & Todman D (2001), *War Diaries, Field Marshall Lord Alanbrooke,* Weidenfeld & Nicholson, Londo, ISBN 1-84212-526-5

*Ellis L (1946), *Welsh Guards at War,* Gale & Polden, Aldershot

French D (2000), *Raising Churchill's Army,* OUP, Oxford, ISBN 978-0-19-924630-4

*Foot MRD (1966), *SOE in France,* HM Stationery Office, London

*Foreman D (2008), *To Reason Why,* Pen & Sword, Barnsley, ISBN 978-1-84415-792-1

Hitchens M, (1992).*West Downs – A Portrait of an English prep School,* Pentland Press, Durham, ISBN 1-872795-76-5

*Hill J (1991), *China Dragons,* Cassell, London, ISBN 0-7137-2275-4

*Ions E (1972), *A Call to Arms,* David & Charles, Newton Abbott, ISBN 0-7153-5620-8

Keegan J (1982), *Six Armies in Normandy,* Penguin, London, ISBN 0-14-00-5293-3

Lindsay M (2000). *So Few Got Through,* Leo Cooper, Barnsley, ISBN 0-85052-754-6

*Masters J (1956), *Bugles & A Tiger,* Michael Joseph, London

Maule H (1976), *Caen,* Purnell, Abingdon, ISBN 0-7153-7283-1

McKee A (1964), *Caen – Anvil of Victory,* Souvenir Press, London,

McIntyre (2005), *Royal Berkshire Regiment,* tempus, Stroud, ISBN 0-7524-3471-3

Mead R (2007), *Churchill's Lions,* Spellmount, Stroud, ISBN 978-1-86227-431-0

*Morgan F (1950), *Overture to Overlord,* Hodder & Stoughton, London

*Morley R (1966), *Responsible Gentleman,* Heineman, London,

*Murrell N (2011) *Dunkirk to the Rhineland,* Pen & Sword, Barnsley, ISBN 978-1-84884-389-9

*Myatt F (1968), *The Royal Berkshire Regiment,* Baylis, Worcester, ISBN 241-01536-7

Neillands R (2002), *The Battle for Normandy 1944,* Cassell, London, ISBN 0-304-35837-1

*Niven D (1971), *The Moon's a Balloon,* Hamish Hamilton, London

Rostron P (2010) *The Military Life & Times of General Sir Miles Dempsey,* Pen & Sword, Barnsley, ISBN 978-1-84884-252-6

Saunders T (2003), *Operation Epson,* Leo Cooper, Barnsley, ISBN 0-85052-954-9

Stewart A (2011), *Six of Monty's Men,* Pen & Sword, Barnsley, ISBN 978-1-84884-371-4

Stone D (1998), *Cold War Warriors,* Pen & Sword, Barnsley, ISBN 0-85052-618-3

*Vandeleur J (1967), *A Soldier's Story,* Gale & Polden, Aldershot

Warner P (1975), *Stories of Famous Regiments,* Purnell, London

INDEX